In recent years, the idea of 'he(strategy in addressing the c(Unfortunately, healthy agein;   since most older people exper   at some point in their lives. A more realistic strategy is to inspire and coach older people to actively negotiate the challenges of ageing by setting ambitions and achieving appropriate goals. This is exactly what Berit Lewis does in her book Ageing Upwards. By taking on an approach based on the principles of mindfulness, she shows us how to actively embrace growing old.

Frank Schalkwijk – gerontologist,
Leyden Academy on Vitality and Ageing

Ageing Upwards is like a 'Rough Guide' to the most important longevity revolution of our time! As we are all living longer, there is a greater need to be able to navigate the third or even fourth stages of our lives in a way where we can continue to thrive and flourish. Berit's mindfulness-based approaches in this book offer information, ideas, structure and practice that can be easily adopted to really embrace ageing in a positive way with responsibility and choice.

But this book should not just be read as you start to think about ageing; this is an essential handbook in mid-life (or even younger). As a leadership coach I see the constant pressures of complexity and uncertainty in our world impacting the demands, stresses and performance of leaders and their employees. Knowing oneself, conscious cultivation of our strengths, setting goals and ambitions, living and leading into our values, reframing negative thoughts and having a growth mindset are all trademarks of compassionate leadership and thriving organisations. Ageing Upwards considers all these aspects as a key part of mindfulness-based living and ageing. This book is thus an essential companion for all leaders and professionals and for anyone who wants to be able to create connection and engagement and make an impact on healthier workplaces.

This is a great handbook written with a depth of research, real examples, stories and practices (including links to mindfulness recordings). It is a book I will keep returning to, in supporting the leaders I work with as a coach and for my own acceptance, perspective and embracing of my own ageing.

Jacqui Fairbrass, leadership coach and founder of Trafalgar Personal Development Ltd

I was completely absorbed in this book. Berit's clear, engaging voice makes this easy to assimilate. The advice seems simple, paradoxically almost obvious but has never occurred to me before. This was a compelling read. Loved the stories and the summaries (milestones through the map). The reframing of the inevitability of ageing into awareness of a journey where we have choice was powerful, comforting and energising. I turned 50 last year so this doesn't call to me, it shouts.

Anwen Edwards – Senior HRBP at NATO Communications and Information Agency (NCI Agency)

Thank you, Berit, for allowing me to be one of the first to read Ageing Upwards! *Turning ANTs (automatic negative thoughts) into PETs (positive enhancing thoughts) is just one of the gems of practical tips that make this book a delight to read. Embracing the practicalities of getting older instead of complaining about them, proactively teaching our minds to reframe situations so that we grow wiser from them instead of letting them drag us down – this book provides the reader with useful tools that will enable them to move through life (more) happily.*

Berit is a mindfulness coach, mother, adventurer and student who combines her interpretation of traditional secular Buddhist

teachings with today's challenges and academic insights in this book. It is easy-to-read, yet filled with scientifically proven findings that are translated into practical steps that anyone can follow. I do not hesitate in recommending this book to anyone who is looking to go through life thriving. Regardless of biological age, any person who has developed the maturity and interest to investigate the meaning of life will enjoy this book.

On a societal level, I would recommend this book as compulsory reading material for my colleague health care professionals. Our health care systems are struggling with fighting illnesses because we are not helping people enough to develop coping skills that could prevent many of these illnesses in the first place. Ageing Upwards can provide a useful supplement to healthcare interventions
Julia Heidstra MBA – Chief Information Officer,
AmstellandZorg

This book is a must-read for those wishing to remain mentally vital as they age. Berit artfully combines her vast (mindfulness) experience with her recent research to provide a practical path towards resilience, full of wisdom and understanding. Mental vitality is crucial as a basis for ageing upwards and reducing our healthcare burden, next to nutrition and physical activity.
Brenda Childers – former CEO, Amsterdam Institute of Finance, currently researching exercise in older individuals at Leiden University Medical Centre.

One of the greatest transformations in human history is occurring right now, yet few even know about it. With Ageing Upwards, Berit Lewis will give you awareness about this transformation and the incredible life opportunities that await you. This new reality of ageing dramatically rewrites our Life Map by adding a new phase of healthy, active, relevant and even profitable life. With this book Berit will provide you with the awareness, mindsets and practices *you will need to reimagine your own life map and make the years ahead your very best.*

Paul Long – founder of New Way Forward

I love how this book is the antidote to all the anti-ageing messaging we're bombarded with, particularly women. I'm also a big fan of the practical and mindful approach. Well done, Berit, this book is so thought provoking and gives us all a great path to follow.

Catherine Garrod – author of *Conscious Inclusion*

As someone approaching the expected retirement age, and someone who wants to make the very most of the years ahead, I read this book with hope and interest. Berit has written a useful and positive book. She presents a credible argument for the huge benefits of mindfulness. She has robustly curated relevant research to demonstrate the benefits of the book's approaches and suggestions to help age upwards. Berit has the gift of being able to explain intangible concepts and to then offer practical, easy to apply ways to enable the reader to take helpful actions. I particularly found useful the chapter summaries and the embrace model. There is also the opportunity to practise and develop the skills she shares in the book through activities and guided meditation practices. I noticed that after I read the book I felt mentally more positive. This was an unexpected benefit that demonstrates the power of Berit's book.

Krista Powell Edwards Fellow CIPD MA –
author of *Credible HR: A handbook for communicating credibility in any situation*

Once we realize that our thoughts and emotions are as independent of one another as they are intertwined, we can willingly choose to separate them and pay more attention to what it is we want, rather than what it is that has happened to us. Old age, being the burdened topic of modern societies, is an excellent reason to explore mindfulness as a tool for greater contentment. Berit has done an excellent job at resourcing and providing all the necessary skills for ageing with more awareness, acceptance and self-compassion.

Micaela Bartels – initiator of PR:OUD, a Dutch pro age movement.

A mindfulness-based framework for the longevity revolution

Ageing Upwards

Berit Lewis

First published in Great Britain by Practical Inspiration Publishing, 2023

ISBN   9781788604338   (print)
        9781788604352   (epub)
        9781788604345   (mobi)

To protect the privacy of the individuals, the names of mindfulness course participants have been changed and in some cases the contexts of their stories has been altered.

Want to bulk-buy copies of this book for your team and colleagues? We can customize the content and co-brand *Ageing Upwards* to suit your business's needs.

Please email info@practicalinspiration.com for more details.

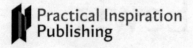

CONTENTS

PROLOGUE

'*Embrace the suck of growing old!*'

Those were the words one of my previous military colleagues at Danish Defence blurted out to me, with a big smile on his face, on my 30th birthday. The phrase 'embrace the suck' is usually something soldiers say to face the horrifying realities of war head-on. It is used to confront situations, no matter how unpleasant or uncomfortable they might be. My colleague was in his mid-sixties, about to retire and suffering from quite a few health problems. The phrase made sense to him. To him, age meant facing pain, loss and death – the same as if he was going to war. I was young and in a very different place in my life. I was fit and healthy. Getting old was something somebody else was doing. If I was tired, it was because my two young children kept me awake at night. I didn't understand why it would suck to grow old. The future was bright and promising.

But the phrase struck a chord with me. Although you might not be going to war, there is still plenty that sucks as we get older. Pain and suffering is inherent in living. Sometimes we even like to put ourselves in situations where we will experience pain. Some of us like to watch horrifying, dark Scandi noir crime series. My son plays VR games where he is attacked by dead zombies. A common way to create discomfort for ourselves – which is even encouraged by health authorities – is to exercise. We pursue university degrees or take on stressful jobs that may involve many uncomfortable hours of learning and maybe hard physical work. Or we decide to have children, which provides us a never-ending supply of unpleasant experiences, from the gruelling nights awake when they are young to the eternal negotiations about bedtimes and basic hygiene when they are older. I have often wondered why we are lured towards this discomfort. Why do soldiers choose a job where they have to be prepared to embrace the atrocities of war? The answer I came up with is that life would be very empty and meaningless if it consisted purely of hedonistic pleasures. Giving birth, for instance, was one of the most profound events of my life yet, at the same time, the most painful thing I have ever experienced. My life wouldn't be the same had I not chosen the pain.

It is not that each of us purposely wakes up and asks *'how can I make myself suffer today?'* Yet we accept that there is rarely any gain without pain. When we play a game, we set out to win, but it wouldn't be fun playing if we knew we would win every time. If that was the case, there would be no challenges to overcome and no rewards to be had. Similarly, the possibility of failing at the things we do in life has to exist or else life becomes rather empty. We want to be able to make a difference, have an impact on something or help someone. The paradox of all this is that although we know deep down that difficulties are unavoidable and the source of meaning, purpose and pleasure, we still find it hard to accept that they are a natural part of life.

When my 50th birthday began to approach, I decided to investigate the 20-year-old invitation to embrace the suck of ageing. As a mindfulness teacher and a student of ageing and vitality, I was intrigued by the encouragement to embrace ageing rather than, as we are mostly told by society, resist it. According to Collins dictionary: 'If you embrace a change, political system, or idea, you accept it and start supporting it or believing in it.' It also means to hold someone (or something) 'tightly, usually in order to show your love or affection for them'.[1] That sounded like a very peaceful and mindful way to approach the last part of life. I was also curious to see if ageing is as bad as its reputation suggests. Does it really suck to grow old? And, finally, I wondered what one can do on a practical level to embrace ageing? This book is my investigation into all those questions.

PREFACE:
WHAT TO EXPECT FROM
THIS BOOK

TAKING RESPONSIBILITY FOR YOUR OWN LIFE AND AGEING

In this book, I set out to meet the challenges that longevity creates in society by exploring what each of us can do to take responsibility for our own life and ageing process. The world is currently experiencing a profound transformation in what it means to be a human being. On average, people can expect to live about six years longer than their grandparents did,[2] and it is expected that by 2050 newborns will be able to look forward to 100 years of living.[3] What a gift! How are we going to spend those extra years we have been given? On the other hand, the increasingly ageing population is seen as a challenge, and the question on everybody's mind is how we are going to sustain our healthcare and welfare systems with the alarming decrease of the proportion of working-age people in the population. The total age dependency ratio is projected to rise from 56.0% in 2021 to 82.6% by 2100.[4] The 'system' – the politicians, the employers, the health and medical care industry as well as the insurance companies – is scrambling to find ways to face this new world. However, in the end, true and sustainable change must come from within each one of us, as part of the system. While the longevity revolution requires a change in the way we organize our societies, it can also be a catalyst for us to shift our mindsets and improve the way we live our lives. Not just the last phase of our lives, but all of our lives.

The book is inspired by the experiences I have gained over 10 years of teaching and practising mindfulness. In particular, I draw on the experiences I have gained from creating and teaching the eight-week Mindfulness Based Vitality and Ageing (MBVA) course as well as carrying out qualitative research into the effects a mindfulness practice had on the participants. I did this in cooperation with Leiden University Medical Centre and Leyden Academy on Vitality and Ageing in the Netherlands. This work has taught me that when we start to practise mindfulness, we acquire some essential qualities and skills for making the most of life and ageing. Those are important because, in the end, each one of us is responsible for our own happiness. Although we cannot take responsibility for *what* happens to us, we are accountable for *how* we respond to it. We cannot sit and wait for the discrimination that is happening to older people to end, for instance. Of course, we must actively work to end it in due time, but right now we have to navigate in a world that is ruled by it. One way to do this is to become aware of, and make sure that we don't internalize, the stereotypical narrative and let ourselves be limited by old-fashioned and stereotypical views of what it means to be 55 or 95. Likewise, we cannot sit and wait for cures for various age-related declines and illnesses, but we can learn to mindfully respond and adapt to whatever situation we find ourselves in. The sooner we cultivate this way of living and the skills required for it, the better equipped we will be, as individuals and as a society, to face the challenges and opportunities of the longevity revolution.

I am not promising to give a one-size-fits-all solution to happy ageing. There are many ways to create a good life. I recently went on a retreat at a Zen Buddhist monastery to explore if this tradition could teach me something that my mindfulness practice hasn't given me. The words of the wise abbot at the monastery, Tenkei Coppens Roshi, supported me in finding my way. *'There are many ways to play a violin'*, he said. Each one of us must find out what works for us. However, I believe we are in dire need of 'violin teachers' who can show us various ways to play and can support us in finding our personal tune. Despite the copious amount of research and literature on ageing, there is a gap regarding inspiration, insight and practical strategies that can empower us as older individuals to handle the process of adaption and enable us to continue living satisfying lives despite age-related difficulties. I believe a mindfulness practice can help us. It doesn't prescribe how we should live our lives. Rather, it can provide an impetus for us to explore our inner and outer lives and, based on what we find, make conscious decisions on how to make the most of our newly given longer lives.

This is a personal book, and you will find a lot of my own personal reflections in it. While it is an invitation to practise mindfulness, it is not a step-by-step self-help book for learning mindfulness. As a matter of fact, you might have more questions than answers after reading it. It is my aim to shake up the way you think about your age and life by telling you some stories, referring to research studies and interviews with both spiritual leaders and ageing experts.

The framework I will introduce you to gives the scaffolding that will allow you to start finding your own answers. If you have done a mindfulness course before reading this book, then you are well prepared, and this book will give you some new angles and insights. If you are new to mindfulness, don't worry! You will still be able to follow the book, and I will give you the fundamentals to get started. I hope this book will be an inspiration for many readers to seek out mindfulness and try it for themselves beyond this book, or to expand their practice beyond the basic introduction workshops they might already have tried. If you decide to do so, I recommend joining a course with a qualified teacher so that you will have the necessary support and ensure your commitment. Mindfulness cannot be understood by reading a book. One needs to feel and practise it with both the intellect and the body.

I also hope to reach leaders and professionals aiming to cultivate, attract and retain a diverse, mature, experienced workforce, or healthcare professionals whose jobs involve assisting older people in finding ways to continue living rich, fulfilling and productive lives.

MINDFULNESS 2.0

Mindfulness has become mainstream over the last 12 years. It is being taught everywhere – in schools, workplaces and hospitals. This is a great development, but unfortunately it has also led to a reduced, capitalistic version of mindfulness, adapted to time-deprived, stressed-out people and the egocentric attitudes of the Western world. Sometimes this is referred to as 'McMindfulness', a play on words from fast-food culture.[5] It is limited and a misinterpretation of both the original Buddhist mindfulness teachings and the evidence-based secular version introduced to the West in the shape of courses such as mindfulness-based stress reduction (MBSR) or mindfulness-based cognitive therapy (MBCT).[6] McMindfulness is easily accessible and requires very low engagement. Unfortunately, it has led to a lot of misconceptions or half-truths about what it is to be mindful. One of these is that mindfulness is relaxation. *'This is my way of being mindful'* is something I hear regularly, often referring to an activity that makes the person relax and gives them a break from everyday life. This usually involves something like cooking, playing music, gardening, doing puzzles or sports, or simply just looking out the window. And, yes, there can certainly be a mindful element to all these activities, but more often than not when we do these things, we are allowing the mind to wander, which is the opposite of being mindful. For instance, when we are cooking, we might think about what happened earlier that day or start to plan tomorrow's dinner. Don't get me wrong, relaxing and doing the things we love is very good for our health and well-being, but it is not mindfulness.

I have come to view mindfulness as a continuum. At the bottom end of the continuum lies the skill of being able to choose a focus point and sustain attention and concentration. The benefit of this is improved concentration. Very often, guided meditations that help us concentrate also make us feel relaxed, which is why people associate mindfulness with relaxation. And it certainly has some benefits. When we focus on the present moment, our bodies and mind step out of the busy doing and achieving mode, and this allows us to just 'be'. Our autonomous nervous system goes into a calm mode where we can rest, digest, heal and connect.

The parasympathetic nervous system takes over from the stress-induced fight/flight/freeze sympathetic system, where we focus on achievement and/or danger. A balanced nervous system is important to our health, and it also allows us to make wise, calm decisions. Therefore, just a few minutes of mindful meditations during the day can be extremely helpful.[7]

There are benefits as we move up the mindfulness continuum, and the more we invest, the more health and well-being can be gained. As we move up, we not only benefit from being able to control and sustain our attention but also start to become more aware of our habits and behavioural patterns. These patterns stem from the way we are wired genetically and from our social and cultural upbringing. With this awareness comes freedom to respond in conscious ways to whatever happens. We gain better emotional understanding and control. We learn to meet our lives as they are, including the pain and discomfort, with acceptance and kindness. This is where one would hope to get to if participating actively in the eight-week MBSR course. Though keep in mind that the learning process is lifelong. The more we meditate and act mindfully, the more it becomes a habit and a way of living. When I started to practise mindfulness meditations, I put alarms on my phone to remind me on a regular basis to pause and notice what is going on in my mind and body. This process has gradually become more intuitive, and I am now able to pause naturally from time to time. For even more experienced meditators, mindfulness becomes a trait. In 2016, Daniel Goleman and Richard Davidson reviewed the available research on meditation and found that the more hours we meditate, the greater the benefits we reap. At some point, the hours of meditation result in altered traits that can be observed not only in our behaviour but also in brain scans, as physical changes occur in the brain.[8]

The framework set out in this book will take you up to or beyond the middle of the continuum, because this is where I, as a secular mindfulness teacher, feel equipped to teach you and where I invite you to aim if you want mindfulness to truly help you cope with the challenges that come with ageing.

The mindfulness I teach is evidence based. I come from a Western academic background, and I prefer to consult scientifically valid research before venturing into something. Mindfulness breaches many academic walls – biology, medicine, psychology and physiology, to mention a few. It can also be placed somewhere between a religious and spiritual practice on one side and a secular, scientific, evidence-based approach on the other. I lean more towards the secular than the spiritual. Having said that, out of curiosity, and while doing research for this book, I dipped my toes into the spiritual side. For instance, I went on a Buddhist Vipassana retreat, which involves 10 days of silence and intense mindfulness meditation. That put my secular teaching into perspective, and I will share with you some of the insights from the experience where it is relevant to this book. This is in no way with the intention of convincing you of a certain belief, but rather to challenge myself and seek inspiration for what could be gained by going further up the continuum. I leave it up to more experienced spiritual teachers to guide those of you who would like to venture further that way.

To receive insights in life, we need the time and space to step back from our everyday. We need to allow ourselves to tune in to, feel and listen to our bodies and reflect on what we experience and feel. No matter where you are in life, I hope this book can inspire you to take a pause and make space for inner contemplation and reflection. I do not believe there is a right or wrong way of ageing. Don't let the many books on 'successful' ageing mislead you into thinking that someone else can define what it means to be successful and what is important to you. There is only your own perception, response and adaptation to a continuous process of living. However, by following the ageing upwards framework in this book, you will be better equipped to find your own way.

HOW TO READ THE BOOK

After the Introduction, the structure of the book falls into three parts. The first part includes a discussion of what it means to age well (Chapter 1) and an introduction to the ageing upwards framework (Chapter 2).

The second and third parts of the book investigate the ageing upwards framework in more detail. In Part 2, I introduce the foundational mindfulness *loop*, by which I mean setting aside time to practise paying attention (*notice it* – Chapter 3), labelling our experiences (*note it* – Chapter 4) and consequently improving our awareness (*know it* – Chapters 5–7). 'Know it' is discussed over three chapters: Chapter 5 focuses on gaining awareness of what drives our behaviours; Chapter 6 investigates our self and abilities to change it; and Chapter 7 looks into being aware of a purpose in life.

In Part 3, I build on the improved attentional control and awareness we gain by going through the loop regularly, and I suggest ways to utilize it (*embrace* it) to respond to the challenges of living and ageing. The title of Part 3, 'eMBrACe', is written as a mix of lower case and upper case letters in an acronym that emphasizes key terms associated with the second part of the framework. 'M' stands for choosing our Mindset (Chapter 8). 'Br' stands for Broadening our perspective to embrace difficulties (Chapter 9). 'A' stands for meeting challenges with Affection for oneself and others (Chapter 10). 'C' stands for Committing to actively adapting (Chapter 11). The 'e's at the beginning and end of 'eMBrACe' represent the continuation of the mindfulness loop (described in Part 2) which forms the basis for us to embrace our lives.

In Chapters 3–11, I refer to research in the area and also draw on my own experiences and those of past participants of my mindfulness courses. Furthermore, I credit a range of ageing, mindfulness and meditation experts. At the end of each of these chapters, you will find a recap of the chapter and recommendations for recorded guided meditations which will help you practise the aspect in question. You can access the recordings simply by pointing your phone to the provided QR codes. At the end of the book, you can find a list of all the available recorded guided meditations, which are available from www.ageingupwards.com.

INTRODUCTION

THE PARADOX OF AGEING

Tell me, are you young or are you old? It's a trick question, of course, as it is all relative and depends on who we compare ourselves to and the situations we find ourselves in. Yet as a society, we persist in thinking that people belong to one side or the other. It is time to challenge our collective story about ageing and stop looking at it as a binary. It is not that we are either young or old. We are somewhere in between, depending on the context.

The narrative of our society claims that by default a younger person is somehow better, healthier, happier and more successful than an older one. This cultural obsession with youth, however, can easily mislead us into wasting our happy senior years longing for youth. I recently turned 50 and I received a lot of well-intended but ageist jokes that would mock, pity or comfort me for my age, implying that it's all downhill from here. As if life is a mountain to be climbed, with hard work, excitement and valuable and rewarding achievements for the first part, followed by a sad, unfulfilling descent and decline once we have passed the summit. But what if I tell you that the age at which we are the happiest in life is actually 80! I am referring here to the U-shaped happiness curve, which visualizes the repeated research finding that people, across countries, deem themselves to be pretty happy when young, are much less happy in their fifties when going through the infamous midlife crisis, and become increasingly happier as they continue to age.[9] Something doesn't add up here. As a 50-year-old at the bottom of the curve, why would I strive to stay young when statistically my level of happiness will go up with each birthday I celebrate? The title of this book is a reference to the U-shaped happiness curve and a dismissal of the myth that it is all downhill from the age of 50.

'AGEING' IS ANOTHER WORD FOR 'LIVING'

I once interviewed a professor about her research on the influence of psychological factors on physical symptoms. Being interested in ageing, I asked how her research is relevant for older people. She surprised me by saying that she is not really interested in the process of ageing. In her experience, people differ a lot in their capacity to cope with their situations, but this is not age dependent. *'A person is a person'*, she said. The professor makes a good point here. While age certainly is a determinant of happiness, as the U-shaped curve indicates, it is just one among many.[10] My own mindfulness teacher and mentor, Kathy Ward, had a similar reaction when I asked if I could interview her on how mindfulness can prepare one for ageing. She said, *'I don't know if mindfulness can prepare you for ageing, but it can prepare you for life.'*

'Ageing' is just another word for 'living'. Let's say I find myself staring into an open fridge and realize I have forgotten what I was looking for. My inner ageist voice might call this *'a senior moment'*, but this is just what happens to a brain that is overloaded with 6,000 thoughts per day.[11] Come to think of it, if a senior moment equals forgetfulness, I think my 16-year-old son has a lot more senior moments than I have. The determinant of a happy life is not the age we are at when we experience challenges like forgetfulness, but rather how we respond to them. This is great news, as it means that the effort we put into learning how to cope and live well when we are younger will continue to benefit us throughout life.

Instead of a mountain to climb, I would rather let my life resemble a scramble up and down many hills, with valleys, detours, roundabouts and viewing spots along the way. Or, as the British philosopher Alan W. Watts points out, life should not be considered a journey, because journeys have an end destination, and although life does have an end, it is not about getting to that. Instead, he suggests we look at life as a piece of music or dance, with the process far more important than achieving something at the end.[12]

If life is a dance, then so is ageing. Ageing involves periods of transition that we have to dance our way through, just like any big change that happens in life. Whether it is becoming a teenager or turning into an adult, ageing involves leaving past roles to enter a new one. It can create an identity crisis involving instability, confusion, frustration and possibly even depression and anxiety. This is perfectly normal.

I was thrown into an identity crisis in my thirties when my husband was offered a job in the Netherlands. In the beginning, it was a great adventure. I was living in an different environment in a new country with interesting new people and cultures; and I got to spend time with my young children. But the honeymoon period wore off and I found it hard to identify with my new role as a stay-at-home wife and mother. I realized that I had lost a big part of my identity when I quit my career as a communication consultant in

Copenhagen. Transitions are never easy or pleasant, but we always come out on the other side. We might not be better off or worse off, but we will always have changed in one way or another. I believe that the key to steering a transition in a positive direction is to meet the challenges with curiosity rather than resistance and to acknowledge that life is impermanent. In my case, I decided to go back to university to study psychology, which eventually steered me towards mindfulness. I could have focused on all the things that were missing in my new life, but instead I chose to focus on one of the things that truly matters to me: continuing to learn.

I danced my way through that 30-year transition. It was one type of dance, and I now find myself moving to the rhythm of a different kind of dance in my midlife transition. Ageing will be a particularly challenging dance, I am sure; but I have confidence that my precious dance experience will benefit me. I sometimes hear people say that age is just a number. I don't agree with that. My age is an important number, and it has great influence on how I behave and how I see myself. I am also, however, much more than my age. To dance through age includes finding a balance between acknowledging our age and at the same time not letting it be the only thing that defines us. And throughout the process we need to remind ourselves that it is the dance itself that is important, not the end.

I AM NEITHER YOUNG NOR OLD – I AM HERE NOW

I invite you to visualize yourself standing on a linear timeline with your past to the left and your future to the right. I am aware that some people visualize time as back to front instead of left to right, but the idea is the same. I imagine you are probably somewhere in the middle or past the middle on the timeline. If you are like most people, you spend a lot of energy resisting the older you and wishing to be further towards your youth. I hope this book will help you connect with wherever you are right now on the timeline and meet this moment with kindness and acceptance as best you can. By taking this approach, you will be cultivating the ability to cope with whatever lies in the future, simply because your ability to be in the present moment will continue to slide along with you as you get older. Your journey does not consist of you jumping from one box with the label 'young' or 'middle-aged' to one that says 'old'. Rather, it is an infinite succession of presents moments. I believe that this perception and the ageing upwards framework I am about to introduce you to will help you make the most out of each of these moments.

PART 1

FROM STRIVING TO THRIVING

Yesterday I was clever, so I wanted to change the world. Today I am wise, so I am changing myself.

—Rumi

CHAPTER 1

FROM SUCCESSFUL TO MINDFUL AGEING

WHY DO WE AGE?

'You look the same!' That's what we all said to each other when my friends and I got together after several years apart. It was a lie of course. Each of us had more grey hairs and sagging skin. I found myself going along with this collective deception, but afterwards I wondered why. What would have happened if I had complimented one of my friends on her slightly deeper and more numerous wrinkles? I am pretty sure she wouldn't have been pleased. I probably wouldn't have been either, if she had pointed mine out. Culturally, ageing is something we fight against. Wrinkles and grey hair are not considered beautiful. We want to look young with smooth skin and firm, slim bodies and lots of colourful hair on our heads. We want to be able to do the same things physically as we did when we were 30 and be as mentally and cognitively sharp. There is no shortage of books, movies, articles or blogs telling us to strive for youth and selling ways to age successfully. But successful in what way? Successful in beating the natural process of ageing?

Let's take a step back and investigate why we age? There is not a straightforward answer to this, but there are two dominating theories for biological ageing in humans and other mammals, each with underlying sub-theories. The overarching theories are known as the *programmed* theory of ageing and the *non-programmed* theory of ageing. The programmed theory implies that ageing follows a biological timetable and is purposely coded into us to cause or allow deterioration and death. This has a direct evolutionary benefit, as ageing gets rid of us once we have reproduced and ensures that resources can be reserved for the next reproducing generation. The non-programmed theory of ageing, on the other hand, sees ageing as an unavoidable adverse side-effect of other biological functions. One of the sub-theories of the non-programmed theory of ageing is the *wear and tear* theory, which intuitively makes sense: just like a car gradually wears out through use, so do humans. The *antagonistic pleiotropy* theory by George Williams is an example of a wear and tear theory. It states that we carry certain gene variants (alleles) that have multiple effects (pleiotropy) which enhance our health early in life but then become harmful (antagonistic) to us later in life. The genes responsible are in the so-called *selection shadow*, as their harmful effects only occur after the reproductive phase.[13] In other words, traits which are expressed late in life are not passed on to the next generation as they are 'hidden' when the selection process happens. One out of many examples of this is the high level of testosterone in male humans, which increases fitness in early life but gives higher risk of prostate cancer later in life. Scientists are still researching and discussing which of the theories are most valid,[14] but the mere fact that we do not know the reason why we age is an invitation to reflect on our mindsets about our own life and death. How we perceive the reason for why we age is critical to how we respond to our own ageing process. If we believe in the programmed theory of ageing, it will be hard to motivate ourselves to live healthy lifestyles, as we will still face a herculean battle against a genetic death mechanism. If, on the other hand, we understand that ageing is much more complicated and could be a side-effect of something else, it means that there are more buttons we can push to influence the process.

So, what decides your individual ageing process? As you might expect, this is also very complicated and is yet to be fully understood. From a biological point of view, scientists have identified nine cellular and molecular hallmarks of ageing, which together determine the observable characteristics of ageing.[15] However, these biological hallmarks, what influences them and the interactions between them are not straightforward. We all know that a person who has smoked, eaten unhealthily and gotten no exercise will look different to one who has had a healthier lifestyle. But there is more to it than life choices. Your genes, and whether you have lived a life that has turned certain genes off or on, have tremendous influence. Psychological factors influence our ageing in terms of behaviour, cognitive function, sense of identity, perception and attitude. Social factors such as available resources and cultural norms also either speed up or slow down our biological ageing process.[16] Biology, psychology and sociology might be separate research disciplines, but when it comes to how to create a thriving ageing life, they are of equal importance. Nevertheless, we often limit our judgements of successful ageing to biomedical criteria.

SUCCESSFUL AGEING: ONLY FOR THE ELITE OR LUCKY FEW?

Ageing successfully lends itself to various interpretations. First, there is the difference between our chronological and biological ages. We cannot influence our chronological age, as it is simply the amount of time that has passed from our birth till now. Our biological age, however, depends on various biological and physiological factors – genes and lifestyle, for instance – as well as psychological and social factors – skills for coping with difficult emotions and navigating social relationships, for instance. Most people think that the lower this number is, the more successful you are in ageing. Preferably, your biological age should be the same as or lower than your chronological age. Our biological age can be measured as an objective state of being at a certain moment in time. This can be assessed using different biological markers. Two popular ways are measuring the methylation of your blood (methylation does the same to your cells as rust does to metal) or measuring the length of your telomere (the caps of the chromosomes, which shorten every time cells divide).

If you are a medical scientist who wants to find ways to understand and slow down the biological ageing process, it makes sense to use such measurements to evaluate whether or not your intervention or drug is successful. For the rest of us, however, successful ageing as an objective optimal state of being can easily create frustration. While it is possible to slow down our biological ageing process by living a healthy lifestyle, at some point our efforts will be in vain. No matter how great our genes are, how much exercise we do or how much money we throw into anti-ageing creams and anti-inflammatory smoothies, it is a battle we will lose sooner or later. In other words, 'successful ageing' is an oxymoron, and we are setting ourselves up for failure when we aim for it.

What if we replace the word 'successful' with 'healthy', as is often done in more recent books and articles on ageing? Rudi Westendorp, Professor of Medicine of Old Age at the University of Copenhagen, Denmark, laughed when I suggested this. He said: '*Ageing is when our health declines – so how can ageing be healthy? There is no such thing as healthy ageing.*' Merriam-Webster's definition of health supports Rudi's observation. According to this, being healthy is 'the condition of being sound in body, mind' and '*especially*: freedom from physical disease or pain'.[17] If this is the definition of health, how can the term possibly describe a period in our lives that is often accompanied by decline, pain and illness?

Having said that, I have talked to many older individuals suffering from various chronic illnesses, injuries or disabilities who still classify their lives as 'healthy' or even 'successful'. This is backed up by a group of researchers at Leyden Academy on Vitality and Ageing in the Netherlands who reached out to citizens of Leiden aged 85 years and older. Only 10% of the 599 participants satisfied all the criteria to be classified as 'successfully ageing' (based on quantitative scores for physical, social and psycho-cognitive functioning as well as well-being); yet when asked about their ageing, the majority believed themselves to be successfully ageing, and on average they gave themselves eight points out of 10 when asked to rate the quality of their lives.[18] This study illustrates the so-called *disability paradox*, according to which people can feel good despite disease, disability and handicap. There is obviously more to a good ageing life than focusing on how to stall the biological ageing process and prevent dysfunction. In the Leiden study, the participants valued well-being and social functioning more than physical and mental functioning. Similarly, in a study from the University of Illinois Chicago, 153 persons, of all ages, with disabilities were interviewed, and the researchers observed that their quality of life was dependent on finding a balance between body, mind, spirit and social relationships. In other words, they found that when parts of the body stop working, it is possible to compensate by using other available resources and to thrive despite, or in some cases even because of, a disability.[19] [20]

The message here is that so-called successful or healthy ageing is not just for the lucky few who don't have any physical or mental health challenges. The narrative that our well-being will automatically slide downwards once our functional abilities start to decline is simply not true. Both the U-shaped happiness curve and the repeated findings that the disability paradox exists prove this. It is clear that a thriving ageing life depends on more than biology, physical health and functioning.

A LESS DICHOTOMOUS APPROACH TO AGE AND HEALTH

Older people have some extra challenges relating to the strong societal norms around age. In recent times, the spotlight has been on mitigating discrimination based on race, gender, religion and sexual orientation, to mention a few. Discrimination based on age is another 'ism' we need to confront – *ageism* refers to stereotypes, prejudice and discrimination towards others based on age, and unfortunately it is very common. A 2020 survey of 83,034 people found that one in every two held moderately or highly ageist attitudes (such as negative stereotypes and prejudices), and out of the 57 countries that participated in the survey, 34 were classified as moderately or highly ageist.[21] This is beneficial for neither society nor us as individuals. Self-ageism, or internalized ageism, is when these societal beliefs are turned inward so that we limit our own abilities and possibilities. The World Health Organization (WHO) recently released a report on ageism, which gives a long list of serious consequences for ageing individuals, based on research. This includes a shorter life span, poorer physical and mental health, and slower recovery from disability and cognitive decline. Furthermore, ageism reduces older people's quality of life, increases their social isolation and loneliness, restricts their ability to express their sexuality and may increase the risk of violence and abuse against them. The report also claims that ageism can contribute to poverty and financial insecurity for older individuals, and it estimates that ageism costs society billions of dollars.[22]

The challenge is that ageism is often not recognized as a problem. We are simply not aware of it, because it is so commonly accepted and ingrained into policies, laws, institutions and even our language. Just take the word 'elderly'. This puts 727 million individuals into the same box, as if they make up one homogenous group.[23]

Interlinked with ageism is *ableism*, as a loss of some abilities is common with age. Ableism is the discrimination of and social prejudice against people with disabilities, based on the assumption that people with a disability require 'fixing' and that they have a lower quality of life than able-bodied persons. As we have just seen with the disability paradox, this assumption is simply not true, yet in society we have this idea that human beings need to be a certain way to be classified as 'normal' or healthy. Take the WHO's definition of health: 'a state of complete physical, mental and social well-being and not merely the absence of disease or infirmity'.[24] The term 'complete' implies that one is either 100% healthy or not, but if you are anything like me, there is always something that can be improved. If someone had asked me this morning whether I was in a state of complete physical, mental and social well-being, I would've said no – my back was aching, my legs were stiff and I felt tired. Now, this afternoon I feel much better, and I would be inclined to answer yes, though many hours of being alone with my book has left me feeling a bit lonely. As with all things in life, our health and well-being are continually changing. Struggling, feeling discomfort, suffering from pain or being less able to do something is part of life and completely normal. It doesn't necessarily justify being categorized as unhealthy or old. It just makes us human. I believe it is our ability to thrive throughout the ups and downs of life, with pleasure and pain, that truly defines us as being healthy and alive.

With this book, I invite you to take a less dichotomous approach to ageing and health. Life is not straightforward. People are not either young or old, healthy or unhealthy, able or disabled, victims or perpetrators of ageism. Most of us are a mix of all of these. To face the current societal narratives on ageing, we all need to step out of automatic pilot, explore our potentially stereotypical thought patterns and find new ways to engage with life.

MINDFULNESS CAN HELP US ADAPT

Rita was a student of the MBVA pilot course I taught. She is a good example of how we can benefit from stepping back and taking a new perspective on life. She was an active and healthy yoga instructor and had always imagined that yoga would enable her body to stay strong and flexible. However, at age 63 she started to have pain in her shoulders and arms due to calcification. This was a major cause of frustration for her. She started to worry: *'What if I am not able to continue yoga? Will my body end up weak and frail?'* Her image of her future self as a healthy, flexible, physically strong 80-year-old faltered. Practising mindfulness, however, gave her the tools to adapt. Instead of sitting down and ruminating over the things she could no longer do or worrying about the future, she took a step back and looked at what it was that yoga gave her in the first place. She started to explore other ways to gain the same pleasure, meaning and sense of identity. Tai chi was one of the alternatives she came up with. Her mind was no longer occupied with worries about ageing. *'I know now that health is also in the mind'*, Rita reflected. *'I am not so worried about ageing any more... I will not just focus on how my body will be when I get older. I also have other things that can keep me strong.'*

The idea for the MBVA course sprang out of observations made by my supervisors Professor David van Bodegom and Frank Schalkwijk at Leyden Academy on Vitality and Ageing, with whom I collaborated when doing my master's thesis on vitality and ageing. They believe the one-sided efforts of biomedical science to stall the ageing process and prevent dysfunction should be broadened to include investigations into how to inspire, coach and empower older individuals to continue living satisfying lives. My personal and professional experience as a mindfulness teacher made me hypothesize that mindfulness could be an intervention that would give ageing people exactly that – a set of tools, or rather a way of living that would empower them to live rich lives in spite of (or maybe even because of) age-related disabilities and challenges.

I had very promising research to lean on. In the last 20 years, mindfulness has received increasing interest due to the wide range of observed benefits. Previous studies indicate that mindfulness can help reduce stress and worry,[25] loneliness, depressive feelings[26] and systemic inflammation, and it can improve mental health,[27] sleep,[28] awareness, self-efficacy[29] cognitive functioning and psychological well-being.[30] Although most research into mindfulness has targeted young or middle-aged adults, the benefits I just mentioned are highly applicable to older individuals who are dealing with a large range of potentially stressful financial, mental, social, emotional and physical challenges.[31] Despite the obvious potential, surprisingly little academic attention has been paid to the plausible benefits of mindfulness in older individuals.[32] However, the research that has been carried out is promising. A 2019 review of the existing knowledge on the effects of meditation training on healthy ageing indicates that meditation practice delays the onset of dementia, improves cognitive functions, reduces anxiety, depression and stress, and promotes positive emotions.[33] Some research suggests that mindfulness might reduce our biological age too.[34]

The result of my research on the MBVA course confirmed my hypothesis. After having practised mindfulness for eight weeks, the participants (aged 55–74) described themselves as more flexible in their views and behaviours. They started to focus less on the things they could no longer do, and more on the things in life that gave them pleasure, meaning and satisfaction. They also described how mindfulness had given them a way of perceiving and acting in the world that allowed them to better negotiate the challenges of life and ageing. Specifically, they found it helpful to regularly pause, step back and meet whatever life brings them with awareness, openness, acceptance and self-compassion. Mindfulness seems to be able to help us age well by enabling us to develop an accepting, flexible mind.

Having a flexible mind means that you put yourself in control. Not in terms of what happens to you, but rather how you respond it. This sense of control is important to our well-being, as illustrated by a recent study which took a closer look at the disability paradox. The study found that the most consistent factor for well-being despite substantial functional decline was whether a person felt in control.[35] The ageing upwards framework, which I will introduce in the next chapter, will help you gain this control.

CHAPTER 2

FROM AVOIDING TO EMBRACING AGE: AN INTRODUCTION TO THE AGEING UPWARDS FRAMEWORK

GIVING NEW LIFE TO AN OLD KITCHEN KNIFE

Imagine you are cycling down the road on a crisp autumn day. Suddenly, your left foot loses its grip, and you tumble to the ground. You manage to get back up uninjured, but realize upon closer inspection that one of the pedals has fallen off your bike. What do you do? You take your bike to a bike repair shop, of course! You get it fixed and, voila, you are back on the road again. This is how we fix most of our problems. We look for the broken part and fix it, and then all is well. Most people see age-related challenges the same way – individual parts start to break down through wear and tear, so we try as best we can to fix them. Maybe it will take a new knee, a new hip or a pacemaker before the person 'works' again. But because the parts are starting to get close to their use-by date, they get harder and harder to fix. This has consequences for other parts too. As a result, the person no longer works – the machinery is faulty and no longer has purpose. Is this the way you view older people – or yourself? Let me suggest an alternative which focuses on what matters to us instead of what is the matter with us.

Imagine an old kitchen knife. The shaft has gone a bit grey and furrowed. Unfortunately, the blade has become so dull that it is pretty much impossible to cut through any vegetable with it. Would you call it faulty? Probably, as it no longer does what it was created to do. What use is a knife that cannot cut? The blade needs to be sharpened or replaced, or potentially the whole knife needs to be discarded. This is a mechanical way of looking at things, and there is nothing wrong with it. It is after all a very successful philosophy underlying science, and the reason why we have found ways to live much longer. But let's try looking at the knife from the philosophy of functional contextualism. '*Say what?*' Yes, it is a bit of a mouthful, and it's not a philosophy we read about every day. The meaning is in the name: it considers the context in which the knife needs to function. Maybe the knife no longer needs to be used to cut vegetables. Maybe instead it could be used to crack garlic or nuts using the flat part of the blade. Or it could be used as a safe prop in a theatre production. Or you could use it to clean your nails or scrape the ice off your car windows. In all these very different contexts, the knife still has a purpose. It can no longer be described as broken, faulty, obsolete or dysfunctional. Do you see where I am going? What would happen if we started looking at ageing through the philosophical lens of functional contextualism instead of from the traditional biomedical mechanical point of view? What if we could be more creative and flexible by seeing our lives in a different context, not just according to how we saw ourselves when we were younger?

That is the mindset we're going to cultivate in this book. Mindfulness is a major part of the so-called *third wave* of behavioural therapy. It is in contrast to traditional Western psychotherapy, which is built on a mechanical philosophy and has symptom reduction as its goal. The third wave of therapy does not look at people as if there is something 'wrong' with them. There is nothing that needs to be 'fixed'. The view is based on the observation that ongoing attempts to get rid of 'symptoms' create more suffering and that these usually return, sooner or later. Mindfulness, on the other hand, teaches us that the urge to control or avoid difficult thoughts and feelings is largely responsible for our problems and that as long as we are fixated on trying to control how we feel, we are trapped in a vicious cycle of increasing suffering. The purpose of therapies based on functional contextualism is not to get rid of our suffering, but to help us accommodate it as part of our rich and meaningful lives. This accepting approach is highly beneficial to our well-being and mental health. Functional contextualism rests on a substantial and continually growing amount of evidence.[36] To experience age-related illness, pain or decline in one or more faculties does not mean that we are broken or dysfunctional. Like a well-loved knife, we just find ourselves in new contexts that are open for us to discover.

NOTICE IT, NOTE IT, KNOW IT, EMBRACE IT!

I hate to be the bearer of bad news, but you will most likely find yourself in plenty of challenging contexts in which you will get to practise this new approach to life. Individuals born in the European Union in 2019 can expect to live, on average, 81.3 years.[37] Unfortunately, you can also expect that of those years, only 64.2 will be in good health.[38] The healthy life expectancy (HALE) measured at birth gives the average number of years a person can expect to live in 'full health', without disease or disability. Most of the years you spend without full health will probably be at the end of your life. And, furthermore, age-related illnesses rarely come alone. Statistics say that from the age of 65, the prevalence of *comorbidity* increases. Comorbidity is a medical term which describes the presence of two or more diseases or medical conditions in the same patient. The likelihood of comorbidity is 60% for people aged 75–79 and more than 75% for those aged 85–89.[39] Medical statistics on ageing provide dire reading material, but such is life. It is not my aim to improve these statistics, but to tell you that you have the power to meet them with a strong and flexible mindset. That is the good news!

As mentioned earlier, as part of the research for this book, I went on a 10-day silent Vipassana meditation retreat. This was led by Mike Helmle, who has spent seven years studying and practising meditation in Thailand in isolation and under guidance of Buddhist scholar Anthony Markwell. In one of Mike's talks (the teacher does not have to be silent), he introduced us to the concept of dukkha. This is often said to mean 'suffering', but a more correct definition would be 'discontentment', 'discomfort' or 'dissatisfaction'. Life contains a lot of dukkha, but the teachings of Buddha can help us liberate ourselves from it; the way to do this is to see the body and mind as two separate things. Mike says that *'pain is physical, suffering is mental'*. By this, he means that pain is all the inevitable hardships and pains that will occur in our lives, whereas suffering is our interpretation of and identification with the pain. It is our instinctual, but optional, mental reaction to it. If we can recognize and accept that dukkha is part of life, we can let it become a source of growth rather than suffering. The hardships of life aren't a condemnation or something to get rid of, but rather an opportunity to find joy and meaning in life. Likewise, ageing is not to be mourned, but rather welcomed as an opportunity to gain a richer and deeper understanding of, and meaning in, life. The way to do this is to train the mind so that it no longer identifies with what happens to the body.

To help us practise this, Mike introduced us to four phases:

- Notice it!
- Note it!
- Know it!
- Let it go!

In all their simplicity, these four phases are both a recipe for how to mindfully approach dukkha and a daily reminder to do so. First, we need to pay attention, to *notice it*. We need to stop for a moment and tune in to whatever is happening in the moment. What kind of physical sensations can be felt in the body? What emotions are here? Maybe they can be felt somewhere in the body too? Are there any thoughts present? The idea is to simply notice the thoughts without getting carried away with them and starting to ask why we are feeling the way we are. Next, we give the experience a label. We *note it*. You can, for instance, say, *'I'm noticing stiffness in my joints'* or *'there is a feeling of sadness present'*. We try to isolate an experience from others to see it more clearly. As we are doing this, we start to see repetition and patterns in our experiences and behaviours. This is when the next step naturally arises. We start to *know it*. We gain awareness – you could even say wisdom. Finally, we need to *let it go*. We thank our bodies and minds for the lessons they give and try as best we can to let the newfound awareness lead the way we interact with life and make conscious choices. We don't need to be Buddhists to live according to these phases. The third wave of therapy, mentioned earlier, encourages us to do the same, helping us approach challenges with awareness, acceptance and a flexible mindset that allows us to respond in new ways.

The four phases form the foundation of the ageing upwards framework, which I am about to introduce you to. The first three – notice it, note it and know it – are basic mindfulness skills that are fundamental for the last one – let it go; these are deeply dependent on each other. I have illustrated them as being in a loop, as they are to be seen as pauses throughout our days when we can step back and tune in to notice, note and know what is happening in the moment.

Once we start to notice how our inner world works, we attain better knowledge, and with that we gain the freedom to respond to life in new ways. Instead of intuitively resisting changes and dukkha, we can start to appreciate and fully embrace all that life has to offer. I have changed the wording of Mike's last phase from 'let it go' to 'embrace it', as I have found that 'letting go' can easily be misunderstood as either giving up or moving on in life without taking any action.

To *embrace* ageing, we practise four skills, referred to in the acronym eMBrACe:

- 'M' stands for choosing our Mindset;
- 'Br' stands for Broadening our attention to embrace difficulties;
- 'A' stands for meeting challenges with Affection for oneself and others;
- 'C' stands for Committing to actively adapting.

The 'e's at the beginning and end of eMBrACe represent the continuation of the mindfulness loop. We notice, note and know a moment in life, which we can then embrace by choosing our mindset, broadening our attention, meeting challenges with affection and committing to actively adapting. The effect of this will form another moment to notice, note and know, and so on. You can see the framework as a process of iterative learning. The loop allows you to see the situation more clearly, and by embracing it, you can respond in a way that will benefit your well-being. The framework probably makes more sense when drawn like this:

eMBrACe

The ageing upwards framework depicts ageing not as a stepladder leading to an end state, but as a continuous, skilful process of noticing, noting, knowing and embracing life as it comes. Nothing in life is permanent, and life does not stand still as we go through this loop. Each trip around the loop is a moment, and each moment enables us to continue to live, learn and grow – to age upwards. This forward motion is illustrated by the arrow in the last 'e', moving us onwards and upwards. The framework is an invitation to live our lives as a continuous line of moments, illustrated as:

eMBrACeMBrACeMBrACeMBrACe

In the following chapters, you will find a more detailed description of each of the phases and inspiration for how you can start to cultivate the relevant skills. Although the phases are based on mindfulness, I will occasionally include some tools outside of what is traditionally associated with mindfulness – for instance, skills that help us to endure commitment and behavioural change or tools to assist us in cognitively reframing our thought patterns and beliefs. Mindfulness is not a panacea, but it is a great place to start.

PRACTISE, PRACTISE, PRACTISE: INVEST IN A THRIVING (AGEING) LIFE

The ageing upwards framework requires patience and practice. It takes a lot of effort and time before going round the loop of the framework becomes a habitual way of living. However, this is the case for pretty much everything that is important to us. We all know that we must invest in our relationships, for instance. Happy marriages don't just happen effortlessly. We like to say that with age comes wisdom, that older people are wiser. And, yes, studies have found that our emotional intelligence does improve as we age.[40] Older adults, for instance, report better regulation and greater control over their emotions. Negative emotions have also been found to decline in frequency and last for shorter periods. Furthermore, older adults tend to express anger outwardly less often and have better inner control of anger, using calming strategies. Mindfulness traits (sometimes referred to as *dispositional mindfulness*) have also been found to increase with age,[41] with older people having higher emotional well-being because of this.[42] But this doesn't happen automatically for all of us. The majority of us must work for it; there is always more to learn and we can always improve the ways we navigate in life.

Practising mindfulness can help you in your current life, but it is also an investment in your future. It can be part of your retirement plan. Just as you make sure you have enough money saved up to put food on the table and keep a roof over your head, you also need to make sure to keep your mind flexible for the changes to come. Though this book is about ageing, it is not just for people who have lived long lives. The younger we are when we learn mindfulness, the more years of benefit we will have from it and the more opportunities we will have to practise it. I invite you to see all the small annoyances that life brings us as gym equipment that allows us to practise and strengthen ourselves for potentially harder challenges to come.

So, let's get started. Make yourself a cup of tea, get comfortable, open your mind and join me in stepping out of automatic pilot.

PART 2
NOTICE IT, NOTE IT AND KNOW IT

The quieter you become the more you are able to hear.

—Rumi

CHAPTER 3

NOTICE IT: TRAIN YOUR ATTENTIONAL CONTROL

PAY ATTENTION: INVEST YOUR MENTAL CURRENCY WISELY

It is Tuesday morning and the first thing you hear is the sound of rain on your window. You shudder as you imagine how you will soon be getting wet and probably cold too. You pull yourself together and leave the bed, feeling the cold air as your legs meet it. You brew your morning coffee on autopilot only to realize that you have run out of milk. The coffee tastes bitter, and while you drink, you give yourself a verbal flogging for not buying milk. You don't notice, but your body is tense and tight, and your shoulders are up around your ears. You get into the shower pondering what else might go wrong today.

Let's reimagine this scenario.

It is Tuesday morning and the first thing you hear is the sound of rain on your window. You stay in bed for another five minutes, listening and savouring the warmth of the duvet. You take a moment to notice the signs of another day beginning. The smell of rain, the sounds of your neighbours showering, the sounds outside. You get up and put your feet into your soft slippers. You notice the sweet, nutty smell of coffee as you brew it, and despite the lack of milk this morning, you take a moment to truly taste the coffee. You consider that maybe you should change your habit and leave the milk out in the future. When you enter the shower, you feel your body relax as you pay attention to the soft, warm feeling of water on your body. You wonder what kind of opportunities and experiences the day might bring.

Do you see the difference? A lot can change based on where you place your attention.

When I ask people to mention some of the abilities that they believe lead to thriving lives, they never say the ability to shift their attention. Yet attention is our mental currency, and where we choose to invest it sets the tone for our days. The scenario above illustrates three tendencies in our attention: wandering off and not being in the present moment; focusing on the negative rather than the positive; and not noticing the physical sensations and messages our bodies and emotions are sending us. These tendencies not only make us miss out on a lot of the good stuff in life, but also repeatedly spin us into a downward spiral of unnecessary negative thoughts, worries and regret. The secret to a thriving life is the ability to be able to choose one thought over another, as this will influence the emotions and physical sensations that follow. To do this, we need to notice them first. In this chapter, we look at the first foundational skill of the ageing upwards framework: *notice it*.

Note it

Notice it

Know it

A WANDERING AND NEGATIVE MIND KEEPS US SAFE

I am going to ask you to close your eyes for a moment and start counting slowly in your head. Every time a thought pops into your mind, go back to one and start over. Have a go now.

How far could you count before a thought came to mind? Some of us only get to two before we are interrupted, while others manage get to 20. The purpose of this exercise is to get you to experience how incredibly busy our minds are and how easily we can get distracted from being in the moment.

Our minds like to wander. Back in 2010, the psychologists Matthew A. Killingsworth and Daniel T. Gilbert of Harvard University did a groundbreaking study. Using an app installed on participants' smartphones, they tracked 2,250 volunteers ranging in age from 18 to 88. At random intervals, the volunteers were asked to report what they were doing currently, whether they were thinking about their current activity or about something else, and how happy they were. The study found that the participants spent 46.9% of the time thinking about something other than what they were doing and that this led them to score their levels of happiness very low. In fact, the researchers concluded that '*a wandering mind is an unhappy mind*' and that the frequency with which our minds leave the present moment is a better predictor of happiness than the activities in which we are engaged.[43]

It makes sense when you think about it. If our minds are not in the present, we cannot be happy. We might be living fulfilling, rich lives, surrounded by caring friends and families, but if we are too busy ticking off 'to-do lists', or worry about losing it all in the future, we are not present mentally to appreciate it.

So why do our minds wander off? It's because the default setting of our brain was not wired in a way that benefits our mental well-being. Instead, our brain is hardwired to ensure our survival. It has evolved to constantly scan our environment for potential danger to keep us safe. Our ancestors didn't have the luxury of taking a moment to enjoy the present moment, because it wasn't safe for them to do so. We do have that luxury, but we are still walking around with a brain similar to our ancestors'.

Another way our brains protect us is by prioritizing negative stimuli. This is called the *negativity bias*. Try to recall a time when you had to perform. Maybe it was making a presentation to co-workers, playing a piece of music, or cooking a meal for some guests that you wanted to impress. Most likely, the things that you remember best are the things that didn't go so well. Why? Because it's the things that go wrong that you need to learn from. Attending to the positive things is unwise from a survival point of view. If our ancestors were too engaged in the appetising look, smell and taste of the dinner cooking on the fire, they would have risked ending up as dinner themselves.

Life is different now, and it is not just about survival. The good news is that although we are born with the same default wiring as our ancestors, our brains are also extremely flexible. Thanks to *neuroplasticity*, which is the ability of the neural networks in our brains to change, it is possible to reorganize some of our default response mechanisms in the brain so that we can thrive as well as survive.

Let me point out that the mind's wandering is not a bad thing altogether. Apart from keeping us safe, it can also bring us pleasure. I personally enjoy reminiscing over lovely times or daydreaming about a holiday or events coming up. I also benefit from letting my mind wander when I run, as it distracts me from the hardship of exercising. Mind wandering also helps me find solutions to problems or come up with new ideas. The lesson here isn't that we should enforce attentional control all the time, but that we are able to choose when we want our minds to wander and when we want them to stay present.

FORMAL AND INFORMAL ATTENTION TRAINING

To control where we place our attention and rewire our brain so that it works in a way that is more beneficial to our well-being, we need to train the mind as if it is a muscle. We can train our attention in two ways. The first way is through *informal mindfulness*, which is mindfulness without meditation. This is when we notice our experiences in everyday life and deliberately refocus our attention when we wish to do so. This can be done with pretty much anything you do consciously in life: '*How are my mind and body reacting to this meeting I am about to go into?*' '*How does my body feel as I am bending it to touch my toes this morning?*' The second way is to take time out to practice *formal mindfulness*, either while sitting, lying or moving slowly for a certain amount of time. This can be for anything from five minutes to many hours. We often see mindfulness and meditation referred to as the same thing, but it is more complicated than that. You can be mindful without meditating, and you can meditate with intentions other than being mindful.

Formal mindfulness meditation has repeatedly been shown to improve attentional control, and the enhancement has even been seen in complete novices meditating for only 10 minutes a day.[44] Fewer studies have included older people but, among these, there are some promising results.[45] Even the attention of people with dementia or cognitive impairment appears to benefit from practising mindfulness.[46] One study found that the effect of mindfulness was particularly strong for people over 60.[47] It would seem, then, that it is never too late to start.

Mindful meditations allow us to practise various types of attentional control. We can practise simply focusing our attention on a task or stimuli, or we can practise getting better at sustaining this attention over a long period of time. Lastly, we can practise selecting where we want to place our attention and zooming in or out from there. Like the functions of a camera, we can select a narrow focus on a specific task or feeling, or we can zoom out and have a wide field of attention which allows us to become aware of thoughts, emotions and physical sensations as they come and go. These different attentional focuses can help us deal with various challenges in everyday life. If you experience pain, for instance, you might choose to let the feeling of pain go into the background or, with a wide field of attention, become aware of the variety of neutral and pleasant experiences that co-exist with the pain in the present moment. Or you might choose to focus your attention right on the point of pain and observe and lean into it with curiosity and kindness. Why you might choose to explore pain will be discussed later in this book.

'*But I cannot control my thoughts*', I hear you say. You are right. Thoughts pop in randomly, just as we feel physical sensations and emotions randomly. If you sit still and observe your inner workings, you will see how each moment is a flow of thoughts and sensations appearing, changing and dissolving. So, instead of trying in vain to control these, we give the mind a specific task to do. While it is possible for us to have a wide field of attention, we don't have the brain capacity to zoom in and have a narrow focus on more than one thing at a time. Although we have been told for many years that multitasking is a valuable skill, it is simply not possible for us to focus in detail on more than one task. But we can use this knowledge to our advantage. By giving our full attention to something in the present moment, we occupy the brain's resources and stop it from wandering off. If, for instance, you note that for the hundredth time your mind is starting to go over the same situation – maybe a recent incident where you felt embarrassed about something you did – you can choose to shift your attention to, say, the physical sensation of feeling your feet on the floor. That's it! Give the mind something else to focus on. Note the sensation of your feet making contact with the floor. You might prefer to focus on your breathing or the feeling of your bottom on a chair. It doesn't matter what you pick as long as you use at least one of your senses and bring all your attention to it.

And, yes, your mind will continue to wander off again and again. New distracting thoughts, regrets and worries will continue to disturb you. Rebelling against our hardwiring does not produce a quick revolution. Evolution, as we know, is pretty slow, and it takes time to overwrite instincts. Persistence and patience are key. Whenever your mind goes off somewhere, acknowledge it, thank your brain for doing its best to keep you safe and bring your attention back to your feet on the floor. This is a basic mindfulness skill: notice whatever comes to you, note it by giving it a label, let wisdom arise around it by knowing it for what it is (*'just a thought'*, for instance) and come back to your chosen point of focus. In time, you will find that the effort pays off. You will find it easier to concentrate on a task and stop yourself from getting hooked on useless negative spirals of regret and worry. It is extremely empowering to know that we can consciously direct our attention to where we want it to be.

I invite you to play with your attention. Make it a game, a mindful challenge to see what your mind is capable of. You can explore on your own, but in the beginning it helps to let yourself be guided either by the voice of a teacher or through recorded guided meditations. There is an abundance of guided meditations available via various apps or the internet. Be aware though that these guided meditations are not necessarily based on a mindful approach, and even among those that are, there are different types of meditations, with only some focusing on practising attentional control.

LET'S BE PATIENT REBELS!

The quest to improve our attentional control is not easy. Not only do we come up against strong genetic forces, but also our current way of living hinders us. We are constantly on our electronic devices and easily interrupted by phone alerts. A study from 2019, conducted by a team of European scientists, found that due to the abundance of information we have access to today, we keep our attention on a particular topic for shorter periods.[48] Our attentional control also diminishes with age. Dr. Cheryl Grady and colleagues used functional magnetic resonance imaging on the brains of younger and older adults while they were doing tasks such as reading and found that older adults, especially those over 65, had difficulty activating brain regions necessary for concentration.[49] Other studies have confirmed age-related changes and decline in attentional control processes.[50] We simply get more easily distracted with age.[51]

Still, although it is an uphill ride, we can get better at attentional control through practice. Mindfulness can help us rebel against evolutionary setbacks. While we might not be able to change our genetic make-up, it is possible to change the way we attend to our urges and, over time, overwrite our genetic and cultural preferences for distraction and negativity. While we are not able to control our thoughts, emotions and physical sensations, we can learn to master what kind of attention we give them. With persistence and patience, we can slowly rewire the neurological pathways in our brain. With time, you will find it easier to refocus and sustain focus. It is an important skill to invest in as attention training is a prerequisite for all other types of mindfulness meditations. It is pretty much impossible to practise other mindfulness-based skills if we are not able to focus our attention long enough for us to become aware.

SAVOUR THE PLEASANT

Another informal mindful way to tame the wandering negative mind is to take time to savour the pleasant elements of life. Next time one of your loved ones comes to you for a hug, take a moment to really feel it. The warmth of their body against yours, the soft skin, the pleasant emotions that arise. Or try to drink your first cup of coffee or tea every morning in a mindful way. Use your senses – the smell, the taste, the hot liquid in your mouth, maybe the feel of it moving through your body as you swallow. The more we savour the pleasant moments, the more it becomes a habit. We are literally rewiring our neurological pathways to stop ignoring all the little delights of life. This is a fantastic ability for everybody, but it is especially important for older people as it helps us counterbalance the less pleasant experiences that tend to come with an ageing body.

My 75-year-old mother, Lene Holm Mortensen, is a volunteer at a hospice in Denmark. I once asked her why she likes to spend so much of her time there, assuming it would be a rather sad and depressing job. She told me it is the opposite. She even calls it life-affirming. Viggo Uttrup, a 91-year-old retired priest who used to work with her at the hospice, describes how, as a volunteer, he enjoyed times when some of the residents at the hospice would come together to eat a nice dinner. Together they would savour the small things in life while talking about the big things. These are people who might never have met before, but who are living the last days of their lives together. They connect in the moment over a cup of coffee, a piece of cake, fresh flowers from the garden. They share memories and reflections about life. Life in a hospice can be life-affirming because death reminds us that the little things are not so small after all.

To pay attention to the present moment can give us instant joy, but it can also equip us to handle future challenges. The more we pay attention to our inner and outer worlds, the more we start to understand the relationship between them. By curiously investigating and labeling the things we notice, we start to gain better awareness, which is what we will look into in the next chapter.

START TO PRACTISE: ATTENTIONAL CONTROL

In this chapter, we looked at the first foundational skill of the ageing upwards framework: *notice it!* This deals with our ability to control and sustain our attention. The chapter's main points are:

- We can improve our well-being by choosing where to place our attention.

- Paying more attention to the pleasant and beautiful moments in life can give us richer lives.

- It is possible to overwrite our genetic preposition for a wandering and negative mind.

- *Formal* attention training is time set aside for mindful meditation, and *informal* attention training is paying mindful attention in our everyday life.

- We cannot control our thoughts, emotions and physical sensations, but we can control the attention we give these.

- Choosing and sustaining our attention is a challenge, especially as we get older, but we can get better through practice.

The two guided meditations *Notice it* **and** *Playing with my attention* **will help you practise the skills in this chapter.** To access the audio files, scan this QR code or go to www.ageingupwards.com.

CHAPTER 4

NOTE IT: LABEL YOUR EXPERIENCES

FROM MURKY TO CLEAR WATERS

Sometimes when I teach mindfulness here in the Netherlands, I bring a glass, which I fill up with water from one of the many canals outside and then place on a table at the beginning of the class. I do this to illustrate the interdependence of attention and awareness. At the beginning of the class, the water is very murky, but as time goes on, the sediments start to settle at the bottom and the water becomes clearer. If I were to shake the glass, the water would once again become cloudy. The same thing happens in the mind if we allow it to settle. Suddenly, the nature of the mind will become transparent, and we will gain new insights. The more we practise our ability to consciously place and keep our attention at a chosen focus point, the easier it becomes to observe our minds with clarity. This greater awareness then feeds back to our attentional control in a positive spiral as we learn the nature of distractions and realize that we do not need to get disturbed by them. We can choose to let them float by and return to our chosen point of attention.

An important step for letting our attention turn to improved awareness is to stay with a thought, emotion or physical sensation that we have noticed and investigate it a bit further. The second foundational skill of the ageing upwards framework, *note it*, is placed in the middle of the mindfulness loop to illustrate that our noticing can only lead to knowing if we take the time to pay special attention to what it is that we are noticing.

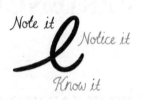

Most of the time, our experiences get muddled up inside us. Thoughts, emotions and physical sensations get mixed in with each other, and it can be hard to tell one from the other. By labelling them, we can learn to see them as separate entities. This makes them less overwhelming, and we are suddenly able to see them as something we can respond to in different ways. Let's take an example that most of us can relate to: relationships with our loved ones. Let's say you call your grown-up daughter to invite her to your birthday celebration. Your daughter tells you that she is too busy to come, and you hang up the phone feeling rather upset. If you take a moment to mindfully investigate your experience, you might start by noting that there is physical tightening in your stomach and chest, tears springing from your eyes, thoughts popping into your mind as you wonder if there are other reasons why she doesn't want to see you. Feelings of guilt, anger, worry or self-pity might come. When you note the experiences you are going through, you will be able to see how your thoughts feed into emotions and physical sensations. You might also be able to recognize some of them as your own behavioural patterns. Patterns that might not have anything to do with this situation, but which are triggered. Noting this will allow you to respond consciously to the current situation.

It is important to point out that by 'noting' I do not mean investigating our experience with the intellect. The intention is not to ask why something is happening or to analyze what to do with whatever it is we are noticing and noting. We are simply observing what is going on in the moment.

Different types of meditation target different parts of the notice, note and know loop. To practise our attentional control (notice it), we usually do *single-pointed meditation*, which is where we keep bringing our attention back to one chosen point – such as the breath, a physical sensation, a sound or a mantra – whenever we notice that it has wandered off. We stay at the noticing part of the loop and use this to practise our attentional control. To gain awareness (note it and know it), we move on in the loop from single-pointed meditation to a more open awareness in which we notice and note physical sensations, thoughts and emotions coming and going. This is sometimes called *insight meditation* or *open awareness meditation*. Kathy Ward is an incredibly knowledgeable and experienced mindfulness teacher who has practised different types of meditation for 40 years. She tells a personal story to illustrate the difference between the two types of meditation. When she was in her twenties, she was introduced to yoga and breath- or mantra-based meditation to help her cope with cancer. She explains that these single-pointed meditations helped her concentrate and cope with worrying thoughts and emotions. '*Meditations distracted me from what was going on in my life, which felt like a reprieve. It felt good.*' However, later in life, as she became familiar with mindfulness, she started to practise insight meditation. '*What I discovered later in life was that my mindfulness practice gives me insight. I missed out on that in my twenties.*' Looking back now, she realizes that although single-pointed meditation can be very helpful on its own as way to escape, it doesn't give you the full benefits of mindfulness. Mindfulness is not about distracting yourself from your thoughts, but rather investigating those thoughts. Rather than escaping reality, insight meditation can make you conscious of your innate and habitual ways of reacting to things, which will give you the freedom to choose to respond in alternative ways.

Stephen Thomas provides another example of how insight meditation can benefit your well-being. He has mastered the art of not getting caught up in what he calls '*the emotional volcano*'. Stephen is 76 years old but looks like someone in his fifties. I met him on a Skype call and was amazed by the virtual energy that travelled from him in Utah, in the United States, to where I sat in the Netherlands. I called him to find out how 30 years of meditation practice, including 30 Vipassana retreats, had helped him in his life. Vipassana is a word from Pali, the ancient language of Buddhism, which means 'seeing things as they really are'. Nowadays, it is also referred to as insight meditation and is one of the main inspirations for secular mindfulness. The Vipassana retreats Stephen attends are taught by S.N. Goenka[52] and consist of 10 days of silent intense meditation and introspection. When I asked Stephen what keeps him so full of vitality, his answer was good genes and diet, but mostly it is because his daily Vipassana meditations taught him to run like an efficient car engine: *'I am not running at 7,000 r.p.m. I am running at an idle of 1,500. My engine is going to last a lot longer.'* Judging from the high amount of energy coming from him, you would think it would be the opposite; that he would be running at a higher speed than the rest of us. But Stephen believes meditation allows him to channel his energy towards what is important and not waste it on other things. *'I have learned to stop and look inside myself and resolve things'*, he says. *'I sit and I observe. Instead of acting out and worrying and fretting, I just observe to see that which is hidden. When I feel some anxiety coming on, I stop and I observe. If I didn't meditate, I would have gone crazy, because I would have worried about this and would be trying to fix that. It is just wasting energy. I have come out of the emotional volcano.'*

PAYING ATTENTION IN A PARTICULAR WAY

To gain insights, we need to pay attention in a certain way. For Dr. Jon Kabat-Zinn, the creator of the MBSR course – the gold standard evidence-based mindfulness course – mindfulness 'means paying attention in a particular way: on purpose, in the present moment, and nonjudgmentally'.[53]

Let us unpack this definition, starting with 'paying attention... on purpose'. To pay attention on purpose means to be aware of being aware. This sounds very abstract, I know, and the following might be a bit difficult to follow if you have never meditated before. It basically means to note what you notice. Let me try to explain using as an example the simple act of walking mindfully. As you are about to take a step, you might notice that your brain is sending instructions to your leg to lift. You might feel the raw physical sensation of lifting your leg, the contraction and release of your muscles, the texture of your clothing touching your skin, your foot losing contact with the ground and so on. But while you are noticing all those things, there is also an awareness of experiencing all these things while moving. You are not just aware of walking; you are aware of being aware of walking. You have an awareness of moving mindfully. Why is this extra level of awareness important? It comes back to what Kathy Ward said in the previous section about the extra benefits we gain from knowing as opposed to just noticing.

You might, for instance, think that you are being mindful when you are playing your guitar or swinging your tennis racquet, because you are very much present in the moment. And to some extent you are. You are present – but you are not present in that certain mindful way. In those situations, I would describe your state of being as *in flow* rather than mindful. The concept of flow is described by psychologist Mihaly Csikszentmihalyi as situations in which we experience a sense of enjoyment, purpose and meaning.[54] When in flow, we are completely absorbed in an activity and forget about time and place. We are challenged at just the right level, doing something that is neither too demanding nor too simple for our abilities. Flow can bring a lot of happiness and is great for our mental well-being. However, it will not allow us to gain the full benefits of the insight that comes with mindfulness, which Kathy and Stephen describe.

Next, in Kabat-Zinn's definition of mindfulness, he asks us to let go of the judgments that naturally arise in our minds with every experience we have. In truth, this is impossible. We are wired to constantly judge the world and our place in it. If you have ever closed your eyes and listened to the sounds around you, you will know that it is pretty much impossible to avoid assessing where the sound is coming from and making judgements about whether you like it or not. We constantly make judgements in order to make sense of the world and to be ready to react if we sense we are in danger. In other words, in practice, non-judging is an unachievable goal. Nevertheless, it is something we should aim towards. It is the intention to not judge that leads to insight. It gives us the astuteness to step out of mechanical reactions and gain the freedom to make more mindful choices.

The intention of not judging is closely connected with another attitude we aim for when practising mindfulness, which is having a beginner's mind. This might sound counterintuitive. You would think that the key to creating a thriving ageing life is to utilize all the experience you have gained so far. And, yes, you are right to some extent; but let's face it, along the way all of us have also picked up one or two bad habits or beliefs that are no longer beneficial.

Marjolijn was 64 when she joined my mindfulness course. During the course, she noticed that she tended to get involved in everything and take it upon herself to solve everybody else's problems. She realized that although her children had grown up and had children of their own, she still took on a mothering role. And it was not just her children and grandchildren she mothered. It was also the man down the road, who she barely knew and who was fully capable of looking after himself. Often this investment in others happened at the expense of her own well-being. By taking a beginner's mind, she engaged in a curious exploration of how she behaved and asked herself how she wanted to live her life in the future. She started asking herself '*is this any of my business?*' Sometimes the answer was yes and she wanted to get involved and help, but a lot of the times the answer was no and she would politely pull back and allow herself to use her energy on the things that mattered to her. Taking on a beginner's mind helps us stay in the present moment and make decisions based on how we experience life now instead of acting according to our own and other people's preconceptions. Having a beginner's mind is particularly important as we get older and our abilities might differ from day to day. We will have good and bad days, and some days we are able to do more than the day before. By approaching each day anew, or even every hour or minute anew, we are able to make mindful decisions.

Now, you might ask, if you must be aware of being aware without judgements and pay attention to everything with a beginner's mind, doesn't that ruin it for you when you are doing something you enjoy? How can that be good for your well-being? What if you just want to relax, enjoy playing your guitar, knit a sweater or create a piece of art? What if you just want to distract yourself from all the thoughts in your head by doing something you love?

Go for it! There is a time and a place for everything, and you will not hear me say that in order to live a good life you must be applying mindful awareness to everything all the time. My advice is to bring a lot of flow and relaxation into your ageing life. There is a time and place for letting our minds wander, for letting ourselves be distracted from difficulties, for being in flow and for going on explorative inner journeys. All the above are useful ways to age upwards. What I *am* inviting you to do is to start becoming aware of these different ways of attending to life so that you can make conscious choices.

FROM RESISTANCE TO HABIT

My Vipassana teacher, Mike, told us that the process of noting and noticing will seem unnatural in the beginning. It is a conscious, and rather tedious, decision to take the time and energy to label your experiences. We therefore need to force ourselves to practise it repeatedly. But over time it will become second nature to us. Eventually, we will automatically note and notice everything we experience.

When you start to meditate, you will also most likely find a strong resistance from your mind and body to just sit still and observe. Being still and doing nothing goes against our instincts, and against how most of us are brought up. One unusual study showed that a significant number of people preferred to give themselves a mild electric shock rather than do nothing for a quarter of an hour in an empty room.[55] Our resistance is partly because we are afraid of what we might find when we look inward. Many of the participants on my course express such fear at the beginning, and it is a very valid concern as mindfulness invites us to face everything, the unpleasant as well as the pleasant. We can easily get overwhelmed by a complete mess of thoughts, emotions and physical sensations. I often get people complaining after the first few sessions of a mindfulness course that they now have even more thoughts than they used to, but this is simply because they are now paying attention to the thoughts. This is normal and OK. The trick is to notice and note them with self-compassion. This is when we can move from noticing to knowing. In the next chapter, we will investigate what kinds of thing we can become aware of and how this knowledge will benefit our well-being.

START TO PRACTISE: LABEL EXPERIENCES

In this chapter, we looked at the second foundational skill of the ageing upwards framework: *note it!* We looked at how attention and awareness rely on and feed off each other. The main points are:

- Attentional control can calm down the mind, allowing us to see more clearly.

- Becoming aware of the nature of the mind can help us control and sustain our attention.

- Mindfulness requires paying attention in a particular way, which involves:

  - an extra level of awareness – noting a sensation is great but noting how we are reacting to the sensation is even more beneficial;

  - the aim to meet whatever life brings us, without judgement.

- Labelling our experiences has to be forced in the beginning, but over time it becomes second nature.

The three guided meditations *Note it – labelling our experiences, Body scan* **and** *Mindful movements* **will help you practise the skills in this chapter.** To access the audio files, scan this QR code or go to www.ageingupwards.com.

CHAPTER 5

KNOW IT: KNOW WHAT DRIVES YOUR THOUGHTS AND EMOTIONS

OUR HUMAN BRAINS ARE CREATED TO MISLEAD US

'Feeling thirst. Intending to drink. Opening eyes. Looking for bottle. Seeing bottle. Intending to reach for bottle. Reaching. Touching. Feeling cold, hard. Intending to lift. Noticing people looking. Feeling judged. Feeling guilt for making noise. Lifting bottle. Noticing weight. Feeling metal on lips. Feeling water in mouth. Feeling pleasure.'

The paragraph above describes the mental notes I made while on a 10-day Vipassana meditation retreat. Have you ever tried to label everything you do, think, sense, feel and experience? It is exhausting, but it pays off as it can give us an awareness of how our minds and bodies operate on a deeper level.

In this chapter, we will look at the third, and last, part of the fundamental loop of the ageing upwards framework: *know it.*

Note it

Notice it

Know it

There are three areas of knowledge that benefit our well-being. In this chapter, we will first examine what fundamentally drives our behaviours. In the next two chapters, we will investigate getting to know our selves and sense of identity (Chapter 6) and our purpose (Chapter 7).

My Vipassana teacher, Mike Helmle, explains that noticing and noting gives us insight into the difference between the *structure* and the *content* of life. A lot of things in life have an underlying structure which sets the rules for how we act. Any language, for instance, has an alphabet, words with meanings, and grammatical rules for how to put them together to make sense. All the things we say or write within that structure is content. The same is the case for sports or plays: there are sets of rules that we follow (consciously or not) and then there is the content we add into the structure. The way we live our lives also has an underlying structure, which most of us are oblivious to. We spend our days getting caught up in content to make sense of the world and find our place in it. We might believe we are in control of this content – how we think, feel, experience and act – but in truth this is controlled by the underlying structure, which is decided by the way our brains, minds and bodies are wired.

I recall giving a talk about mindfulness to an organization once, which I thought went pretty well and I got very positive feedback from the organiser. However, afterwards I read feedback from one of the listeners, who said that she thought it had been a waste of time for her and her colleagues to sit and meditate. She thought that they could have spent their time on more pressing matters. I remember feeling very sad and disappointed. I had even had a pleasant talk with this person over a cup of tea during the break. Why didn't she like me? The fact that I cared so much about what this one person thought of me can be explained in terms of the structure of human beings. For the sake of safety, we are genetically wired to avoid social exclusion. We have a strong urge to be liked and loved by fellow beings. Looking back at this event, I realize that I was caught up in content. I was stuck on a rollercoaster of thoughts and feelings about something that I could not do anything about anyway, not knowing that I was able to step out of it any time I wanted to. If I had been able to see the structure beneath my thoughts and emotions, I would have understood the way the rollercoaster was engineered and could have gotten off the moment I realized I had entered it.

To see the structure takes effort and commitment, but once you do, life will never be the same, because you have looked behind a curtain and seen how it all works. I got a glimpse behind the curtain at my Vipassana meditation retreat. This is an extreme sport for the mind. For 10 days you follow a strict schedule of 45-minute meditation sessions (sitting or walking) starting at four o'clock in the morning and finishing at 10 at night. The living conditions are basic. No communication is allowed – neither with your fellow participants nor with the world outside the retreat.

There is no access to phones, electronic devices, notebooks or books. The reason the retreat is organized like this is that it helps participants become aware of the content they fill their lives with. It is so easy to get distracted. By living like this, I experienced that the potential suffering that I have been running away from my whole life is not as horrible as I thought, yet I have wasted so much time and energy on trying to avoid it.

I realized that a lot of the thoughts that preoccupy my mind are just sensations brought about by my brain or body in order to satisfy some genetically wired needs or desires. Needs and desires that are not all that urgent or which do not need to be fulfilled at all. Take hunger, for instance. I used to have a fear of being hungry, but at the retreat we ate simple vegan food and even skipped dinner altogether. And guess what – I didn't die! Yes, being hungry doesn't feel nice, but I experienced that if I didn't waste my energy thinking about missing out on food, it didn't really affect me. My body quickly accepted it and I learned how to divert my attention when thoughts about food popped into my mind. I also realized that the thought of getting up at four o'clock every morning after little sleep was much more painful than actually getting up at that time. Coping with the cold was the biggest challenge for me, but even so, I discovered that I could still manage to place the unpleasant sensations at the back of my mind and concentrate on other things. In short, I realized that the energy we spend avoiding discomfort is often much more unpleasant than the discomfort itself.

This insight has made it much easier for me to note the times when my 'caveman' brain tries to keep me safe by bringing out various desires or urges in me. I know why fear of discomfort so frequently pops into my head, and I know

I do not need to get distracted by this. I can, at least some of the time, consciously choose to let it pass and dissolve. While I still fall into old patterns, I feel much less controlled by my biological and social conditioning. Looking ahead, I have no doubt that if I manage to keep my practice up, it will help me age well, as I will not get caught up in the pointless content my mind continues to feed me.

KNOWLEDGE OF SELF-CREATED HABITS

When I teach mindfulness to adolescents, I ask them to picture themselves standing in the middle of a field of tall grass. There is a significant restructuring happening in the adolescent brain, consisting of rapid growth of brain matter, formation of new connections and pruning of unused connections. Whenever an adolescent thinks a thought or reacts in a certain way (usually because they have heard or seen others do it), they are moving out into the field and creating various pathways of downtrodden grass. It could be an angry, self-pitying path, based on the thought '*everybody is out to get me*', or a more optimistic path, with the person thinking '*shit happens but I will get through this too*'. The more they use one path, the wider and smoother it becomes, until it is a highway that they will choose for the rest of their lives. Now it is probably a long time since you were an adolescent, but you are still going down the pathways you created then. Do you know what they are? Can you name a few? They have been there for a very long time and they are so downtrodden that you probably don't notice them. You might even consider them to be facts. Most of us think our thoughts are facts, but the truth is that most of them are highly subjective judgements based on emotions.[56] The good news, however, is that although our brains become less neuroplastic as we age, it is still possible to rearrange our inner landscape of pathways. Mindfulness can help us become aware of our personal trails in the grass and start to question them, and then maybe start to make new, potentially healthier ones. We do this simply by choosing to go down new pathways whenever we notice that the old ones are not working for us. With persistence, the new pathways will, over time, become our preferred trails to follow.

Anna, one of the participants on the MBVA pilot course, was able to change her old habit of ignoring her own needs. *'I was a thinker,'* she told me, *'but I was not listening to myself.'* She was 65 at the time and was looking back on a successful career. *'I was going on and on and on but I didn't feel my body.'* As she started to practise mindfulness, she refocused her attention from the head to the body. She began to notice all the messages her body was sending when she was feeling tired or lacking energy. She now has a morning routine in which she does a combination of movements and meditation. This allows her to feel the state of her body and to spend the day accordingly. Some days she has a lot of energy and urges to get things done or socialize, whereas on other days her body and mind ask for rest and quiet contemplation.

It is not a given that the beliefs that served us well when we were younger still fit the body, mind and life of who we are now. For instance, at 40, you might believe that hiking for seven hours is good for you, but at 80, a full day of hiking will probably overexert your body. Mindfulness helps us to listen and adapt continually. A 65-year-old student of mine, Mascha, told me that she had always had a firm rule about not sleeping during the day; this was because she believed it would make her drowsy for the rest of the day and not able to sleep at night. But one day during the mindfulness course, she felt very tired and decided to give her body the rest it was asking for. After 15 minutes of sleep, she woke up feeling much more awake and had renewed energy for the rest of the afternoon, allowing her to engage in activities that made her feel alive. It turned out she had no problems sleeping that night either. She now listens to her body and tries out new ways of living instead of following rigid rules written into her brain by her younger self. Not only is this wise in order to maintain her energy and physical health, but for Mascha it is also an act of self-compassion to listen to and act on the needs of her body.

PRIMARY AND SECONDARY SUFFERING

You are on your way out the door but have misplaced your keys. What emotions come up? Maybe anger and frustration? What thoughts go through your head? Probably a lot of rational problem-solving thoughts like: '*Where did I last see them? Let's try my coat pockets.*' But on top of this, you might notice thoughts of self-blame: '*I am so stupid. Why do I always forget things?*' These thoughts might feed the already existing emotions of anger and frustration. If you take a moment and tune in, you will probably also be able to feel these emotions manifest themselves physically somewhere in the body. Tightness in the jaw and chest? Contractions in the belly?

What tends to happen is that our mind goes down one of our inner pathways. Maybe we start to worry about the future: '*Why am I always forgetting things? Am I getting dementia? My grandmother had dementia. I will probably get it too. What would happen if I got dementia? Where would I live and who would look after me?*' Now you might start to notice other emotions, like sadness and fear. Or your mind might react with fear and anger, and call yourself hurtful things like '*stupid, old, scatter-brained fool*'. Other people might be the target for your anger – your messy partner or your key-eating dog perhaps? By now, you have gotten yourself wound up in a circle of unpleasant thoughts, emotions and physical sensations. Just because of some missing keys. And while you are going around this cycle, your brain has no capacity left to think clearly about where to look for the darn keys.

'*There is a lot of suffering in this world, and we try hard to make it worse,*' Zen master Tenkei Roshi told me with a laugh when I interviewed him. '*We all carry loads in our lives,*' he said, but he also assured me that '*it is possible to have a difficult life and process it well*'. To be able to distinguish between what is happening and the feeling towards what is happening can help us alleviate the load we are carrying. '*Whatever we feel is also a feeling about something. It is not the thing itself.*'

The ability to distinguish between, following Tenkei Roshi, the feeling and the feeling about the feeling is what we gain when we apply a certain kind of attention to our experiences. This is similar to my description in the previous chapter of 'being aware of being aware'. In secular mindfulness teachings, we call this *primary suffering* and *secondary suffering*. Primary suffering is unavoidable. Most of us have lost our keys at some point in life. 'Shit happens' is a rather rude way to put it but, nevertheless, a very accurate description of how unwanted things happen beyond our control. Secondary suffering is our reaction to the primary suffering. It is all the horrible sensations we add to our lives through self-blame and name-calling as well as the catastrophic thoughts and worries about an imagined future. These are all examples of suffering that our caveman brain introduces in an attempt to avoid potential dangers in the future, but those kinds of catastrophizing thoughts are usually not wanted or helpful in today's world.

You might have heard it said, to paraphrase Charles Rozell Swindoll, that life is 10% what happens to you and 90% how you react to it. I am not sure if he had any valid research to back up those numbers, but the message is that the way we respond to things is more important than what actually happens to us. Dr. Russ Harris, an acceptance and commitment therapy (ACT) trainer, invites us to imagine that we have a 'struggle switch' at the back of the neck.[57] By default, it is turned on, which means that whenever we encounter something unpleasant, our first instinct is to struggle against it. We might wake up one morning and discover the body is stiff and aching. With the struggle switch on, the mind is likely to respond with thoughts like: *'What is wrong with me?' 'This is it – life is going to suck from now on!' 'Why can't I just have the body I used to have?' 'How can I fix it?'* It is likely that mixed in with the thoughts, you experience a nice cocktail of emotions like sadness, anxiety and anger, which might very well exaggerate or add to the physical pains in your body. Do you see the vicious cycle? Luckily, it is possible to turn off the struggle switch. We simply notice and note the cocktail of thoughts, emotions and physical sensations, and place our attention somewhere else, as we practised in Chapter 4. You can stop searching for your keys for a moment and say to yourself: *'I have lost my keys and I am noticing a lot of negative self-talk and catastrophizing happening right now. For the next couple of minutes, I will just stand here and pay attention to my feet on the floor.'* When some minutes have passed, you can go back and continue searching for the keys with a calmer and more focused mind. If we don't feed the emotions with thoughts, they will pass right through us. Harvard neuroscientist Dr. Jill Bolte Taylor claims that it only takes 90 seconds for an emotion to run through us. If it stays for longer, it is because we choose to feed it with thoughts.[58]

Holocaust survivor and psychotherapist Viktor Frankl is quoted as saying that 'between stimulus and response there is a space and, in that space, lies your freedom'.[59] A mindfulness practice utilizes that space, as we stop for a moment and pay attention to what it is that is driving our urges, desires, thoughts and emotions. With this awareness we can stop feeding negative cycles, redirect unhealthy inner pathways and lower the secondary suffering we put ourselves through. In the third part of this book, we will look at what to do with this awareness, but before that let's turn to another important type of knowledge that we can gain by noticing and noting: the awareness of who (we think) we are – our sense of self.

START TO PRACTISE: AWARENESS OF WHAT DRIVES YOU

In this chapter, we started to look at the third and last part of the fundamental loop of the ageing upwards framework: *know it!* We specifically looked at knowing what drives you. The main points are:

- All our thoughts, emotions and physical sensations are motivated by socially and genetically wired needs or desires (the *structure* of life). If we become more aware of these, we can make conscious choices about whether to let them rule our lives or not.

- Although our brains become less neuroplastic as we age, it is still possible to rearrange our inner habits and beliefs.

- *Primary suffering* is part of life and unavoidable, but *secondary suffering*, which is our reaction to the primary suffering, is optional.

The two guided meditations *Practising notice it, note it, know it* **and** *The pause practice* **will help you practise the skills in this chapter.** To access the audio files, scan this QR code or go to www.ageingupwards.com.

CHAPTER 6

KNOW IT: KNOW YOUR SELF

CAN I CHANGE MY SELF?

My grandmother used to volunteer at the local nursing home in the village where she lived. She used to describe it as *'visiting the old people'*. She was in her late eighties herself and lived on her own in a small townhouse. As a volunteer, my grandmother would drink coffee and chat with the residents. She did not consider herself to be in the same category as them even though she was the same age as most of them. My grandmother was not alone in feeling like this. In a survey of attitudes to old age, a third of the respondents aged 65 or over said they felt up to 19 years younger than their chronological age, and almost half of the respondents aged 50 or over reported feeling at least 10 years younger than their actual age.[60] How about you? Do you see yourself as 'old'? Or maybe 'middle-aged'? How old is 'old'? Does your own sense about your age contrast with the stereotypes society imposes on you?

Most people I ask say that they are different now to how they were 20 or 30 years ago. I certainly feel different. Sometimes when I look at a picture of a younger me, I feel like I'm looking at a different person. Am I really the same person who in her twenties would wear the same sun-faded clothes for days, sleep in dodgy, flea-infested hostels and not care for much comfort or safety as long as there were new adventures to be had, new places to see and interesting people to meet? Although I still like to travel, I am a bit more driven by comfort and safety today. Are you the same person today as you were when you were younger? While writing this book, I asked my connections on LinkedIn this question, and it hit a nerve. It was clear that people saw themselves very differently to how they perceived themselves when they were younger. It was common for them to think they had grown wiser and more kind, empathetic and compassionate.

In this chapter, we continue to investigate the third and last of the elements of the fundamental loop of the ageing upwards framework: *know it*. We will specifically examine how our perception of our 'selves' – or our 'personalities' (I use these terms to describe the same thing) – influences our well-being.

For a long time, experts thought our personalities became fixed in childhood and were relatively stable from the age of 30. We now know that they continue to be quite fluid and malleable throughout life.[61] This continual process of change that occurs as we age, referred to as *personality maturation*, is seen worldwide. So how and why does this maturation happen, and do we have any influence over it? Can we make ourselves happier by changing who we are?

To answer that question, we need to take a small philosophical detour, because if we need to investigate if we can change our selves, we need to explore what it is that we are trying to change. We need to contemplate what the *self* is, or even if there is such a thing as self. When enduring the hardships of a Vipassana meditation retreat, one of the experiences people wish to have is the dissolvement of one's self. You might wonder why we would want to be liberated from something that for most people is the most important thing in life. The reason is that if you manage to truly 'see' that there is no you, then you can let go of all the thoughts that cause suffering. No more 'me' and 'mine'. No more cravings or attachments to fulfil. Death, illness and pain become much easier to deal with, as they are just realities of an impermanent life, not things that are happening to 'me'. They just 'are'. Admittedly, the concept that a self does not exist is hard to grasp, and I will leave the teaching of it to more spiritual mindfulness teachers who are higher up on the mindfulness continuum (see Preface). Although I am not able to detach myself fully from my self, I am able to see that my sense of self is a construction influenced by the people, circumstances and culture of my upbringing. I therefore also believe that not only can we separate ourselves from our current understanding of who we are, we can also change it and, along with it, our beliefs and behavioural patterns.

HOW TO CHANGE OUR SELVES INTO HAPPIER INDIVIDUALS

While our sense of self is not static, there also seem to be 'core' traits and values that provide consistency in our ways of thinking, feeling and behaving across different situations. So exactly how much can we influence ourselves? To what extent do we inherit our traits, and how far are our personalities connected to our upbringing? Is it down to luck, with some people being unfortunate enough to be stuck with a grim personality and others fortunate to have an optimistic personality? A lot of research has been conducted on the matter, but the findings are not conclusive. The nature versus nurture debate is one of the oldest discussions within psychology. In 2005, researchers Sonja Lyubomirsky, Kennon M. Sheldon and David Schkad suggested the sustainable happiness model, illustrated with a pie chart giving a nice clear indication of what contributes to our happiness: 50% of our happiness is determined by our genes, 40% by our activities and 10% by our life circumstances. Of course, these numbers generated a lot of critique, and even the authors themselves had second thoughts about their claims.[62] The reality is that who we are as people and how we behave is a result of a multitude of tangled forces. The numbers in the happiness pie chart might not be exact, but its broad message still holds: while we cannot change our DNA or the cards that life deals us, we can still influence our well-being via our behaviours. The question, then, is which behaviours should we try to cultivate?

PERSONALITY TRAITS AND WELL-BEING

Meta-analyses, which involve statistical analysis of results from multiple scientific studies of the same thing, indicate that personality traits are one of the best predictors of well-being.[63] Most of these studies base their research on the 'big five' – the five core personality traits of agreeableness (being friendly and compassionate), conscientiousness (being responsible), extraversion (being sociable and enthusiastic), openness (being curious and open to novelty), and neuroticism (being emotionally unstable and prone to negative emotions).[64]

One study from Australia followed 11,104 adults aged 18–79 over a period of four years and found that increased extraversion, conscientiousness and agreeableness were associated with increased life satisfaction, whereas neuroticism was associated with lower life satisfaction. A study from the Netherlands with over 10,000 people participating in a seven-year study came to the same result. The Dutch study also found that changes in personality at one time predicted future measures of well-being. This is interesting as it indicates the direction of causality: it is not our well-being that affects our traits, but rather our traits that affect our well-being.[65]

It is particularly interesting that a large amount of literature names extraversion as an especially strong predictor of well-being.[66] This, however, doesn't mean that introverts are doomed to live unhappy lives. Other traits seem to be just as important. In an attempt to provide a more nuanced perspective, a recent international study went beyond the big five measures to include other well-known dimensions of well-being, which allowed a broader range of personality profiles to be recognized. They found the following five personality traits to be the most predictive of well-being:

1. **Enthusiasm:** to be friendly, sociable and emotionally expressive, and to have fun in life
2. **Industriousness:** to be achievement oriented, self-disciplined, efficient, purposeful and competent
3. **Compassion:** to feel and care about others' emotions and well-being
4. **Intellectual curiosity:** to be open to new ideas, enjoy thinking deeply and complexly, and reflect a lot on experiences

5. **Low withdrawal:** to not be easily discouraged and overwhelmed, and not ruminate and be highly self-conscious.[67]

These do not contradict studies based on the big five, but rather compliment them. The main point here is that while there are multiple personal paths to well-being, there are certain traits that are worth cultivating as they have a large impact on our well-being. So how do we do that?

HOW TO *GROW* OLDER INSTEAD OF MERELY *GETTING* OLDER

The good news is that there are certain positive changes happening automatically to our personalities as we age. Contrary to a stereotypical view that older people are grumpy complainers, research has shown that we develop into more altruistic,[68] trusting individuals[69] with more emotional control.[70] These are in line with the traits I just pointed out as being predictive of well-being. This finding can explain the happiness curve and why our level of happiness goes up as we age.

Some of the changes that happen to our personality are believed to be related to changes in our roles in society. This is supported by *social investment theory*, which states that our personality is influenced by our social contexts and life events. For instance, young adults tend to become more agreeable and conscientious as they grow older, because they take on more responsibilities. While the research on this theory has primarily focused on young adults, there are indications that social investment may influence our personality well into old age, with each year making us more agreeable and conscientious as well as more emotionally stable, but, interestingly, also less extraverted.[71]

Unfortunately, positive personality change doesn't happen automatically for all of us. So, what can we do if we do not like the grey-haired person looking back at us in the mirror and want to cultivate some of the traits that enhance our well-being? This is where meditation and mindfulness come back into play.

In *The Science of Meditation*, Daniel Goleman and Richard J. Davidson[72] refer to a large amount of research suggesting that different types of meditation have different effects on the brain, and thereby different effects on our behaviour and (eventually) our traits. In previous chapters, I talked about meditations that improve our attention and awareness. Other meditations focus on cultivating feelings of compassion and kindness to self and others, which not only is predicative of well-being, as we have just seen, but has also been found to slow down biological ageing.[73] Goleman and Davidson point out that it takes a large amount of practice, as seen in Buddhist monks, to find true altered traits which are visible in brain scans. However, we shouldn't let that discourage us, because they also found that meditating for even a few minutes a day can benefit us. In other words, the more hours we practise a certain type of meditation, the more it will become part of who we are.

Of course, it is not enough to practise on the meditation mat – we need to practise the new version of who we want to be in real life. (We need to practise both formal and informal mindfulness as described in Chapter 3). As mentioned, it is possible to carve new pathways in our brains through sheer persistence. I once decided to be more patient. As part of my daily mediations, I started to silently repeat to myself the phrase '*may I be patient*'. Over time, the phrase crept into my life. When I found myself being tested – usually by my teenage children – I would hear my inner voice reminding me to be patient. It reminded me to pause before reacting. It made me remember the reason why their developing, dopamine-driven teenage brains forgot their promises or did silly things, and I was able to respond in ways that didn't get us into fights. I will admit that if you ask my children, patience is probably not a trait they would assign to me, but I am working on it and improving day by day. We can all pick certain traits to work towards in a similar fashion, which would benefit our well-being. Being more compassionate, curious or sociable are some science-based examples you might practise.

It is on purpose that the title of this chapter has 'your self' written as two words instead of one. 'Yourself' (or 'myself') usually refer to a permanent self that we are meant to be or that we can discover, whereas 'your self' (or 'my self') makes the self something that is separate from us, something that we create and adjust every day in our interactions with the world. So often we ask ourselves *who am I?* or we excuse certain unhealthy habits with *well, this is just who I am*. Coaches and self-help books have told us that they can help us 'find our true selves' or 'find ways to be the best version of ourselves'. The irony is that when we set out with the good intention of 'finding ourselves', we are telling ourselves that we are inadequate as we are and that we need to strive to become the predetermined version of ourselves. But what if we could meet ourselves as we are right now with acceptance and self-compassion? Instead of finding ourselves, we could aim for accepting who we are, but also acknowledging that we are continually *creating our selves*. I recommend replacing the question 'who am I?' with 'how would I like to engage with life?' With a beginner's mind it is possible to choose to nurture the habits and traits of our personality that serve us well in the present and inhibit those that bring us suffering or constrain us. Our selves are neither fixed nor something we need to find, but rather something malleable. Of course, this self-created self must be aligned with what is important to us and our values. This is what we will investigate next.

START TO PRACTISE: AWARENESS OF YOUR SELF

In this chapter, we continued to look at the third and last part of the fundamental loop of the ageing upwards framework: *know it!* We specifically looked at our selves – how our selves are neither fixed nor something we need to find, but rather something that we can actively form. The main points are as follows:

- Studies have found that certain personality traits are good for our well-being. These are enthusiasm, industriousness, compassion, intellectual curiosity and low withdrawal.

- We can purposely cultivate certain behavioural (thought) patterns through formal and informal mindfulness (see Chapter 3).

- *Social investment theory* states that our personality is influenced by our social contexts and life events. Our personality therefore changes as we age.

- Instead of 'finding ourselves', our well-being will benefit from accepting who we are and continually *creating our selves* through the way we choose to engage in life.

The two guided meditations *Exploring my self* and *Identifying personal phrases* will help you practise the skills in this chapter. To access the audio files, scan this QR code or go to www.ageingupwards.com.

CHAPTER 7

KNOW IT: KNOW YOUR PURPOSE

IN SEARCH OF A PURPOSE

'The couch seems awfully attractive when you retire, but you will soon find that it doesn't give you a happy life.' These words come from the 78-year-old coach, author and blogger Herma-Jozé Blaauwgeers. She advises us to stay engaged in life and to find our 'core legacy' as early as possible – preferably before we retire – as it will guide us through this new phase of life. The legacy might or might not be related to your profession. Herma-Jozé's own legacy is simply 'to be a different thinker'. It gives her something important to offer to the world and, at the same time, gives meaning to her life.

In this chapter, we continue to investigate the third and last part of the fundamental loop of the ageing upwards framework: *know it*. We will specifically examine what it means to our well-being to have a purpose in life.

Plato once defined 'man' (a more woke Plato would have said 'human beings') as 'a being in search of meaning'. Making sense of our place in the world is essential to us. It is therefore not surprising that research into happiness and well-being for all ages has repeatedly shown that having a purpose or a meaning in life benefits our well-being in many ways. One study surveyed 7,304 men and women aged 50 and older and found that the more meaningful they found their lives to be, the higher they rated their personal relationships and broader social engagement. They felt less loneliness and had greater wealth, better self-rated mental and physical health, less chronic pain, less disability, greater upper body strength, faster walking, less obesity and healthier lifestyles, including more time spent in social activities and exercise, and less time spent alone or watching television. In addition, they had more favourable biomarker profiles in terms of various objective health measurements.[74]

The research is clear – we need to maintain meaning and purpose in life, and to do so we need to stay engaged. This is a new approach to ageing. In the sixties, narratives of ageing were predominantly about decline and dependency. In 1961, for instance, the social scientists Elaine Cumming and William E. Henry observed that older individuals reduce their levels of activity in things they previously found meaningful. In *Growing Old*, they outline *disengagement theory*, claiming that it is both natural and acceptable for older adults to withdraw from society due to the belief that they have little to contribute to it.[75] There wasn't much empirical support for this theory though, and it was soon dismissed. In response to the critics, Cumming and Henry proposed *activity theory*, which states that active participation in activities and relationships is optimal for healthy ageing.[76]

Both theories about ageing exist side by side today. A lot of people associate older age with a less engaged life, while others see it as an opportunity for being active and engaged in personal interests. A woman once commented on one of my LinkedIn posts that she almost felt embarrassed to say that she had retired and felt 'retirement' had become a dirty word. I can see why she would feel that way, as the word has strong connotations of checking out, being pushed aside and being considered as having less value. The longevity revolution has come on rather suddenly, and our old way of structuring our lives does not match the current demographics of society.

A BALANCE BETWEEN DOING AND BEING

We seem to be caught between two paradigms with a vocabulary that does not do justice to the way of living we desire now. Instead of all of us fitting into the classic three-phase life formula of learning, earning and then retiring, each one of us must find a path which mixes those up in new ways that allow us to continually achieve, earn, rest and learn according to our capabilities.

We talk a lot about work–life balance, but I think we should look instead at finding a balance that allows us to fulfil all our needs throughout our days and throughout our lives. For far too long, we thought that we could get away with working incessantly during the first part of our lives and saving sleep and rest till retirement. I am hoping that the longevity revolution can be a catalyst for a better balance in which we slow down a bit during the first part of our lives, thereby avoiding burn-out or wearing out our bodies too early. According to clinical psychologist Paul Gilbert,[77] three types of emotional system drive us: *threat*, for when we feel in danger and focus on seeking protection; *drive*, for when we strive towards achieving a goal; and *sooth*, for when we rest, heal and give or receive love and care.

During workshops, I sometimes write these three systems on circles of paper. I place them on the floor as a triangle and ask the participants to stand in, or between, the circles of the system(s) that dominate their lives. This is followed by a reflection on how they would like it to be. Very few people want to be living entirely in one of the systems. Too much focus on avoiding danger or striving for achievements will make us stressed and anxious, whereas too much soothing can result in apathy. The majority prefer a balance between the systems, but individuals also have personal preferences towards one of them. Somewhere between the three is our personal sweet spot. This is the place from where we can balance our energy levels, needs and desires. From here, we can work towards a purpose and also have the space to step back and reflect on it. I believe this spot is the foundation for living a life full of vitality.

ADD VITALITY TO LONGEVITY

Vitality is the peculiarity that distinguishes the living from the non-living. It is not reserved for young people, as it is not limited to mere physical energy but also encompasses psychological properties like introspection, enthusiasm, resilience, sense of purpose, self-compassion and spirit.[78] It describes how one can have a chronologically high age without feeling old. It is a highly subjective experience of being alive. A synonym for vitality in my mother tongue, Danish, is *livskraft*, which can be translated into 'life force'. We also see the concept of *life energy* in Eastern cultures. In Chinese, for instance, *chi* or *qi* refers to a force or energy, and it is believed that a proper flow of chi is required to maintain our health. In other words, to have vitality means to be connected to some inner force of motivation that makes life worth living. It is what can get us up every morning despite various forms of discomfort. It is what can make us feel alive no matter our difficulties, pains and disabilities.

Professor Rudi Westendorp and Frank Schalkwijk, who we met previously, believe that if our aim is to enable older people to live lives with a high degree of well-being, it is not enough to prevent age-related disease and strive for healthy longevity; we also need to empower people to take more responsibility for their own quality of life during the extra years they are living. They define 'vitality' as 'the ability of a person to set ambitions appropriate for one's life situation and being able to realize these goals'.[79] I like this practical approach and I believe the way we can set appropriate ambitions is to know our selves well, as we have practised up to now, as well as knowing the things that give us purpose in life. Vitality has the word 'vital' in it. In order to keep our vitality, we must connect with what is vital for us. Each one of us must identify what this is, and it doesn't have to stay the same throughout our lives. You might recall my example of the blunt knife in Chapter 2. Just because we cannot live the way we did when we were younger doesn't mean that we can't find other ways to have vitality. By continually going through the notice, note, know loop, we can ensure that we are setting appropriate ambitions for our life situations and that we do not get stuck in or cling to our old ways.

Do you know what makes your heart sing? What gives you zest in the life you are living right now? It might be hard to define what vitality is, but you can sense if a person has it, and you can definitely feel if it is missing from your life. It is what makes the difference between thriving in life and just surviving. One way of identifying what is vital for you is to work on your values.

KNOW YOUR VALUES

We all have our own values. They are not better or worse than our neighbours', even though they can be quite different. Some prefer to live a comfortable, predictable and safe life, whereas others thrive under more adventurous conditions. It is not the values themselves that make you happy, but rather whether you live a life in accordance with them.

One of Herma-Jozé's values is trust. Trusting that things will be OK, no matter how bleak they look in the moment. She grew up in the shadow of her father, who was a member of the Dutch Resistance and executed on D-Day. Herma-Jozé was born six months later, and her childhood was marked by the loss of her father's affection and a grief-stricken family. Nevertheless, at an early age, she made a conscious choice not to let the loss of her father shape her life negatively, but rather to be inspired by his bravery. Often she repeats to herself: '*My choice was to become a strong woman. I trust that my life is going to be OK. Period!*' This helps her get through difficult times.

Most of us are unaware of our values, and consequentially we are oblivious to whether we live according to them or not, until something feels off. Take Agnes, for instance. She worked for most of her life as a nurse in various conflict hot spots around the world. When she turned 67, her body got too tired for that kind of life, and her children convinced her it was time for her to retire. They found a nice row house in a suburb of Amsterdam, close to where they lived themselves. In the beginning, Agnes enjoyed her new quiet and secure life and spending time with her grandchildren. But soon she got bored and started to feel depressed, which made her physically tired and unmotivated to get up in the mornings. She missed adventure and being able to make a difference for the less fortunate people of this world. Sure, she found a purpose in helping her children and grandchildren in their busy lives, but it wasn't a purpose that made her heart sing. It was somebody else's idea of her purpose. She needed to be part of something bigger. After some soul-searching, she realized that she wasn't living according to her values and this was making her life dull. It took a lot of courage to tell her children that she could no longer help them out as much as she used to. Instead, she approached a non-government organization (NGO) based in the Netherlands, and today she advises NGO volunteers on looking after themselves while caring for others. Her health may no longer be up to living in the middle of war zones, but she feels that she is still part of a community, and being able to contribute is what really matters to her.

THE BIG QUESTIONS

When we, like Agnes, find ourselves in situations which have been more or less forced upon us, we naturally start to reflect on why we are here and what we want to get out of our short lives.

Let me ask you: on your deathbed, which of the following you do wish to utter as your last words? *'I enjoyed it!' 'I made a difference!'* or *'What a journey!'*

Until recently, psychological research on happiness/ subjective well-being was dominated by a strong dichotomy between hedonic and eudemonic well-being. That means either a happy life that aims for personal satisfaction in terms of comfort and joy facilitated by money, time and relationships, or a meaningful life that aims for social contribution, purpose and meaning built on moral principles. Basically, the choice was between finding pleasure or meaning. In 2021, researchers Shigehiro Oishi and Erin C. Westgate suggested a third dimension for what constitutes a good life: psychological richness.[80] Here, the aim is to gain wisdom through a life lived with variety, interest and curiosity, and facilitated through time, energy and spontaneity. Maybe this is a life that is especially worth pursuing as we age and are forced to go through challenge and transition?

It is not, however, the dimension most people prefer. Of 3,728 participants in nine countries who were asked to choose one of the three, most chose a pleasurable life (percentages in the different countries ranged from 49.7% to 69.9%), and this was followed by a meaningful life (14.2% to 38.5%). The least favoured was the psychologically rich life (6.7% to 16.8%).[81] Luckily, we do not have to choose one over the other, but we can aspire to a bit of them all and maybe focus on different aspects in different periods of our lives. Again, our preference is very much connected to our personality and values. Do we prefer stability and comfort, or do we thrive with challenge? The bottom line is there is not only one recipe for a good life, and each one of us will benefit from making time and space for exploring what is important to us. Keep in mind too that there might be other dimensions than the three that scientists have pointed out.

I suggest a fourth dimension for what can constitute a good life: spiritual richness. As we are confronted with the loss of loved ones and get closer to the end of our own lives, it is not surprising that we also start to ask ourselves the bigger questions such as 'what is the meaning of life?' or 'what happens when we die?' Research confirms that our interest in religious and/or spiritual endeavours heightens with age.[82] As Plato wrote, 'The spiritual eyesight improves as the physical eyesight declines'.[83] There is an overwhelming amount of evidence that links spirituality to good health and well-being,[84] so it wouldn't be a bad choice to aim for this fourth dimension. The last phrase we utter on our deathbed could be something like '*I gained wisdom!*'

The aim for a rich spiritual life seems to be the goal for some ageing people. Swedish sociology professor Lars Tornstam developed the theory of *gerotranscendence* – this term is composed of 'gero', as in gerontology, and 'transcendence', referring to his observations of some older people who expressed new ideas that 'transcend[ed] borders and barriers that had circumscribed them earlier in life'.[85] Tornstam carried out a number of large quantitative studies in which a random sample of Swedish and Danish people between the ages of 20 and 104 years were interviewed about their outlook on life, themselves and their relations to others. He found that gerotranscendence correlates positively with age. While not everyone showed all the signs, he identified a group of *gerotranscendent* individuals, who he described as older individuals who developed new understandings of: (1) the self; (2) relationships to others; and (3) the cosmic level of nature, time and the universe.[86] This is in line with an earlier study by Tornstam, in which 65% of Swedes aged 74–100 agreed with the statement 'Today I have more delight in my inner world, i.e., pondering, compared with when I was 50.'[87]

It seems that vitality, meaning and purpose do not have to be found in outward activities. My own mother recently had a realization. She used to get annoyed with my grandmother for wanting to stay at home all the time. My mother would spend the morning getting ready for an outing for the two of them. She would brew coffee, make lunch and pack a picnic blanket. She would then drive to pick up my grandmother only to hear her say that she would rather stay and eat the lunch at home. Now, as my mother is in her seventies herself, she is finally understanding why my grandmother was so reluctant to go out. These days, she too enjoys pottering around in the comfort of her own home making wreaths, reading, writing, gardening and simply pondering life. It doesn't make her any less successful in ageing. We can be so enamoured with activity that we forget we all have different paths to vitality.

PURPOSE AS A TEAM

'*Before you die, please live.*' Tenkei Roshi, who we met in a previous chapter, refers to this quote by the Japanese Zen master Junyu Kuroda Roshi (Hojo-san) when I ask him what one should do to prepare for growing older. He explains that if you have lived a life where you feel like you have fulfilled a task and contributed in some way to the world, it is easier to die. But Tenkei Roshi reminds us that we are not alone in this word. '*We are born as a team*', he says. There is a purpose for us all within that team, and all jobs in the team are important. He compares it to how a hospital functions: '*We can't all be doctors. Someone needs to take care of important jobs like cleaning the windows.*' Also, our purpose does not stay the same. As the needs of the world and our capabilities change, so does our purpose. I believe this is an important reminder to finish this chapter off with. When we talk about finding a purpose in life, it can so easily become an excuse to boost our ego and our status. We might want our name to be remembered for having achieved something grand. But what if we are not living to fulfil our own needs, but the needs of the world? Maybe in our quest for finding a purpose in life, we need to stay humble and focus on the 'we' rather than on the 'I'. Paradoxically, by focusing on others' needs, we can find personal happiness. As mentioned earlier, to give something to somebody is a guaranteed way to feel good. Even with reduced physical and cognitive capabilities, we are part of a team, and just by being present we give to it and fulfil a purpose. To live is a purpose in itself.

We have now looked at the three interlinked mindful foundations of a vital life: notice it, note it, and know it. When we naturally and continually implement this loop in our formal and informal mindfulness practice, we will see the freedom it provides us with. A consciously chosen attention and awareness provide us with the freedom and ability to interact with life in a highly beneficial and flexible way. It provides the scaffolding to fully embrace life rather than just live it on automatic pilot. So what do we do with this awareness? How do we embrace life? It is time to move on to the third part of the book.

START TO PRACTISE: AWARENESS OF PURPOSE

In this chapter, we continued to look at the third and last part of the fundamental loop of the ageing upwards framework: *know it!* We specifically looked at *knowing your purpose*. The key points are:

- It is essential to our well-being to have a purpose in life, and this also makes us physically healthier and live longer.

- A way to ensure that we have a purpose throughout life is to find a better balance between learning, earning and resting every day in our lives.

- The term *vitality* describes a 'life force' within us which is beyond age and physical abilities. We can obtain vitality by setting ambitions that are appropriate for our life situation.

- In order to live vital lives, we need to be aware of what is important to us. Our well-being benefits from identifying our values and living accordingly.

- We all have different paths to vitality. Some value external activities and others prefer more spiritual inward reflections, as described in the theory of *gerotranscendence*.

- A purpose does not have to be something grand. It can simply be being present for ourselves and others.

The guided meditation *Finding zest for life* will help you practise the skills in this chapter. To access the audio files, scan this QR code or go to www.ageingupwards.com.

PART 3
EMBRACE IT!

For after all, the best thing one can do
When it's raining, is to let it rain.
    —Henry Wadsworth Longfellow, 'The Poet's Tale'

CHAPTER 8

CHOOSE YOUR MINDSET

'*I cannot go shopping, I have breast cancer. I cannot visit my friends, I have breast cancer. I cannot....*'

Remember Herma-Jozé, who we meet in the previous chapter? She told me a story about a friend of hers, who we will call Mirjam (not her real name). Mirjam had always tended to focus on the negative things in life. When she was diagnosed with breast cancer, the list of things she couldn't do anymore was endless. But Herma-Jozé found a way for Mirjam to shift her mindset. She sent her a plane ticket to travel from the Netherlands to America, where Herma-Jozé lived at the time. The invitation included participation in a strenuous charity walk, the 'Walk for breast cancer'. Mirjam accepted and the two of them started to prepare, ensuring they were fit and ready for the challenge. The walk turned out to be quite a challenge. For Herma-Jozé that is – not for Mirjam! She walked the walk as if she had never been sick. '*But she lost the argument!*' Herma-Jozé announces with a cheeky grin on her face. '*Now, whenever she comes up with new arguments for why she cannot do certain things, I show her the pictures from our walk, and she is forced to accept that she can still live her life to the fullest. It is all about the mindset.*'

Herma-Jozé's story perfectly illustrates how it matters what we choose to focus on. Do we focus on all the things that we cannot do, or the things we can do? Chapters 9–11 are about our attitude, our perception, the way we frame things – aka our mindset. Just as we can practise attentional control, we can practise attitudinal control.

As you may recall, the acronym eMBrACe reflects the elements of the ageing upwards framework. 'M', 'Br', 'A' and 'C' represent four beneficial ways to bring the awareness gained from the loop into life and respond in ways that allow us to embrace our ageing life. The 'MBrAC' is enclosed by 'e's not only to form the word 'embrace' but also to visualize how a practice of noticing, noting and knowing can be used continually to adjust the ways we respond to life.

eMBrACe

This chapter starts with 'M' for Mindset. It is a general introduction to why it is important for our well-being to consciously choose our perspective on and attitude to life.

eMBrACe

In the next two chapters, I will introduce two specific mindsets that we can benefit from cultivating. In Chapter 9, I discuss the 'Br' for cultivating a *Broad* perspective, as it helps our well-being to see things in a wider perspective. In Chapter 10, I focus on the 'A' for Affection, as a mindset of love, compassion and common humanity benefits our lives and those of the people around us. Lastly, 'C' for Commitment is discussed in Chapter 11, which focuses on active ways to adapt to life.

OUR MINDSET MATTERS

Whether you think life after 50 is better or worse than being younger, you are right. We become what we think. Not only is our perception important for our well-being, as illustrated in Mirjam's story, but it also greatly influences our longevity. In one study, 660 individuals aged 50 and older were asked about their perceptions of ageing. Twenty-three years later, their answers were held up against mortality data, and it turned out that those who had expressed a positive view of ageing lived on average 7.5 years longer than those with more negative attitudes.[88] Professor of Epidemiology, Becca Levy, is one of the researchers behind this study. She has since published a book referring to various studies demonstrating that many health problems formerly considered to be entirely due to the ageing process – such as memory loss, hearing decline and cardiovascular events – are also influenced by the negative age beliefs. She provides strong evidence that the way we think influences our lives.[89]

STRESS AS AN EXAMPLE

How we manage stress provides an excellent example of why our perspective matters and how changing it can greatly influence our well-being and health. You might think that stress is not relevant in a book on ageing. Maybe you assume that when we get to a certain age, we will step off the hamster wheel and get some well-deserved rest instead of spending all of our days working, striving and achieving. This is probably the case for some but not the majority, because stress doesn't stop when we stop working. Stress is a natural feeling and reaction to any difficulty we encounter in life. As age brings plenty of difficulties, stress is also a natural part of ageing.

As the name suggests, one of the aims of the MBSR course is to reduce stress. However, the somewhat paradoxical key learning point of the course is that it is not the stressors themselves we need to worry about or get rid of, but rather our responses. The ability to feel stress is a gift. We have developed a life-saving stress reaction, which is sometimes referred to as fight, flight or freeze. When we sense danger, our bodies will react in a way that will allow us to get away from or fight or cope with whatever might attack us. Of course, today we are rarely attacked by dangerous animals, but that doesn't mean we no longer sense danger. It is just a different kind of danger: *'Did I say something wrong?' 'Will I get cast out of the group?' 'What is that pain in my stomach – is it cancer?'* With the evolution of our brains, and in particular the development of our pre-frontal cortex, we have become much better at imagining dangers. This means that our system is easily triggered to produce a stress reaction, and there is no difference between whether the stressor is a bear, a boss, a friend, physical pain or worrying thoughts about the future. The problems arise when our stress reactions become chronic and we do not have the time between the stressful reactions to recover. Stress can then become harmful and potentially even deadly. Chronic stress can cause many serious health problems, such as depression, anxiety, high blood pressure, abnormal heart rhythms, heart attacks and stroke. Psychological stress has been seen to both mimic and exacerbate the effects of ageing and has an especially negative effect on our immune system.[90]

During an MBSR course, people learn to recognize their instinctual reaction to stress and to stop it by not feeding it with new catastrophizing thoughts. Just like we practised in the foundational loop of notice, note and know in Chapters 3–7. In other words, mindfulness teaches us to change our focus during stress. Instead of looking at it as something to be avoided, we recognize it as a natural part of life, which we have the power to respond to with calm and kind awareness – for instance, by taking a pause and focusing on the breath for a moment. I saw the same skills developing in the participants who did the MBVA pilot course. In my research with the participants, they often referred to mindfulness as giving them a chance to '*reset*' themselves. Whenever they experienced themselves getting caught up in worries, they would sit down for a moment, calm themselves and '*start anew*'.

REFRAME AGEING

Remember my encouragement in Chapter 4 to pay attention to the present moment in a particular way? When it comes to coping with stress, it is not enough to notice and note the feelings of stress; we also need to notice and note how we are responding to it. A lot of the time, our problem is not the problem itself, but the way we think about the problem. It is the same with ageing. Most of the time, ageing isn't the problem – the way we think about ageing is.

The world is a complicated place, and in order to reduce confusion and preserve our limited brain capacity, our brains will constantly attempt to make sense of the world by automatically trying to hang new experiences on pre-existing hooks of beliefs. But those pre-existing hooks might not benefit us anymore (maybe they never did). Also, although we think we are rational human beings, in reality our minds are much more likely to make decisions based on our various innate biases (the negativity bias is just one of many) and our current emotions.[91] In short, our mind does not necessarily have valid beliefs about the world and our place in it, and we cannot always rely on our mind to make great decisions.

Positive psychology is a relatively new branch of psychology. It acknowledges and works with our flexible mind. It aims to beat the negativity bias by turning focus away from our weaknesses and problems. Where classic psychology tends to focus on the things that feel wrong and painful for us, positive psychology pays attention to the strengths, attitudes and behaviours that enable and encourage us to live flourishing lives, though without ignoring the difficulties and pain we also experience. There is a vast amount of research showing that a positive mind leads to resilience, better well-being and better relationships and that it improves health and relieves depression[92] and even leads to longer and better lives,[93] as we saw earlier. The idea of *positive ageing* springs out of positive psychology, inviting us to focus on sources of happiness later in our lives. Just as negative self-talk can be damaging, words of encouragement can motivate us to create better lives. One of positive psychology's favourite tools is *reframing*, which is the process of stepping back and challenging our pre-existing beliefs and thought patterns.

For example, we can reframe the way we look at the ageing brain by replacing the narrative of decline with one of change and transition. Although there is no doubt that age has negative effects on some of our cognitive abilities, most people are not aware that the older brain compensates with an improved ability to see patterns. An older mind might be cognitively slower than a young mind, but it is much better at listening to the messages coming from the senses and emotions before responding.[94] This ability is sometimes referred to as *crystallized intelligence*, a concept introduced by the psychologist Raymond Cattell in 1963. He distinguished between *fluid intelligence* – the ability to solve new problems by relying on skills such as comprehension, problem-solving and learning – and crystallized intelligence – combining learned knowledge with experience to tackle new problems. Research has found that fluid intelligence declines with age, but crystallized intelligence grows.[95] Equipped with this knowledge, we can reframe our view of ageing. Just as the teenage brain is going through a transformation, so is the ageing brain, albeit at a lesser pace and not quite as radically. The main point is that ageing involves transition and not only decline.

To see things from another perspective takes effort. The so-called *confirmation bias* is yet another bias we are born with which hinders our well-being. This is the tendency to favour information that confirms our already existing beliefs. The *mere exposure effect*, also known as the *familiarity effect*, has been shown in repeated studies in which people found certain statements, products, images, taglines and claims more believable simply because they were familiar with them.[96] It is not just the algorithms on social media that make sure we see more information about what started as a small interest or an idea – it is also the way human brains are wired. We simply like repetition. But if we can notice, note and know these biases, we can make a conscious choice to challenge and overcome them. Seeking knowledge and inspiration from reading books, articles, research studies, etc. is one way to question our beliefs and knowledge. Mindfulness is another more inward-facing way. As described in the previous chapters, mindfulness invites us to step out of automatic pilot. To take a beginner's mind and see things as if we are experiencing them for the first time.

Another way to challenge our beliefs and reframe is to talk to other people. My husband, for instance, is an engineer, and I am constantly surprised by how his mind works completely differently to mine. The interchange of different experiences, perceptions and beliefs is also the reason I love teaching mindfulness in groups. It is such a joy to see the amount of reframing and loving support a group of strangers can give each other when put together under safe and supporting circumstances. Sometimes we need someone else to tell us when we have gotten stuck in a particular way of thinking while, at the same time, acknowledging that it is normal to get stuck.

Time can influence our perspective greatly. Stanford psychology professor Laura Carstensen noticed that as we perceive our time left on this earth to be growing shorter, our goals shift. Young people with a long life ahead of them prioritize future-oriented goals, whereas those with less time prioritize present-oriented goals. Carstensen developed the *socioemotional selectivity theory*, based on a great deal of evidence. This states that due to our perception of time, we become more selective in what we deem important. Young adults aim at acquiring information and knowledge to expand their horizons for future-oriented goals, whereas older adults prioritize meaning and positive emotions in the present moment. Interestingly, research on socioemotional selectivity theory has also revealed that older adults pay more attention to, and better remember, positive information over negative information.[97] In other words, as we age, we get better at beating the negativity bias and start to pay more attention to positive stimuli.

TURN OLD *ANTS* INTO NEW *PETS*

Now this all sounds very promising from the chair of a 50-year-old. Apparently, the best is yet to come. According to statistics, I will become a more positive and emotionally intelligent woman. But why do I not see older people with big smiles on their faces, seizing the moment and jumping for joy in the streets? Let's not forget that just because research provides a certain insight, this doesn't necessarily fit with everybody. As Kathy Ward pointed out when I mentioned socioemotional selectivity theory to her, many ageing individuals choose to ignore or distract themselves from the fact that their time is dwindling rather than being motivated by this. Also, the positivity effect doesn't completely cancel out negativity bias. Unfortunately, the negative inner critical voice does not retire when we do.

The inner critical voice is the commentator that has been following you around your whole life, making comments about what you do and what you experience. It is the caveman brain trying to keep us safe and free from potential embarrassment and social exclusion. Its comments can therefore be very harsh and negative: 'You are not good enough!' 'You are stupid!' 'You are fat, wrinkly and ugly!' 'Nobody likes you!' Or they can be more specific beliefs that we repeat to ourselves: 'You are awkward in social situations!' 'You are a terrible cook!' 'You are a bad parent/ friend/colleague/partner/daughter/son!' The critical voice can also come out as rigid thought patterns like overgeneralizing

('*I am always last*'), fortune-telling ('*I will mess this up like I always do*') or mind-reading ('*They think I am an old forgetful fool*'). Each one of us has personal favourites. Psychologists refer to these as ANTs – *automatic negative thoughts*. Just like real ants, ANTs crawl around anywhere anytime, and they eat up our enjoyment of life along the way. Just like real ants, ANTs don't work alone. If, for instance, you get some dates mixed up and miss a lunch appointment with a friend, an ANT might pop by and announce with disgust: '*I am stupid!*' Soon after, other ANTs will join the party with comments like: '*My friend will not want to see me again*' (mind-reading); '*Nobody likes me*' (overgeneralizing); and '*I am going to be lonely*' (fortune-telling). The ANTs will also bring along some familiar emotions like sadness, anger and fear, and you will feel the physical echoes of these in your body. Neuroscience has a saying: 'what fires together, wires together'. This refers to how our neurons create habitual response patterns over time. All it takes to tap in to these pathways is to think one ANT or feel an emotion associated with the ANT and all the ANT's buddies will come out of their holes. When we get older, a special type of ANT joins in. I call them *ageism ANTs*, and they make life miserable by listing all the 'rules' for things you shouldn't do and can't do just because of your age.

So, what do we do with these ANTs? First, we have to catch them (notice them), label them (note them) and acknowledge that they are not assisting us in living happy lives (know them). While we do not have control over our thoughts, luckily, we do have ways to control our attention and our response to our thoughts (as we practised in the foundational loop of the ageing upwards framework). Remember, the point of mindfulness is not to control our thoughts, but to stop letting them control us. Let me illustrate by sharing some of the ANTs that meet me at my desk every morning as I write this book: '*Ah, good morning. Why are you here again? Do you really think you have something to offer the world? You are not a good enough writer! You don't know enough! You are wasting your time. Nobody is going to read this anyway. Go get some coffee instead. Look, cute videos of cats on Facebook!*' No, it is not a great way to start the day. But this is where mindfulness saves me. It helps me to spot the ANTs and hold them lightly. That is, take a step backwards and see them for what they are – just a bunch of negative thoughts passing by. So instead of getting caught up in the inner self-critical dialogue about whether I am a good enough writer or giving in to the urge to run away by watching cute kittens online, I refocus from my head to other parts of my body. I sit for a moment, and I feel and acknowledge the uncomfortable emotions that come with these thoughts. I meet them with other thoughts like: '*Hello ANTs. Thank you caveman brain for trying to keep me safe by urging me to not publish a book that might embarrass me. But I choose to write it anyway, because it feels right and it gives me purpose and pleasure, and hopefully it will inspire others to do what they find important too. It matters to me!*' I turn the ANTs into PETs – positive enhancing thoughts. I change my focus away from the negative things that might come along with this book towards the positive reasons for why I am writing it.

DEFUSE YOUR THOUGHTS

Thoughts are just thoughts. You have no control over them, but you can choose what to do with them. ACT therapists use a technique called *defusion* to get distance from ANTs or other difficult thoughts. Here, to defuse means to detangle your self from a thought. We are not our thoughts, and we do not have to identify with them. To defuse your thoughts, you first need to notice, note and know the difficult thought. As an example, let's use the ANT '*I am too old to…*'. Have a go, you decide what it is you are too old for. It could be '*to wear hot pants*', '*to go interrailing*', '*to start studying*' or '*to change job*' – pick something that you fancy yourself doing. Close your eyes and try repeating this thought to yourself a couple of times. It doesn't feel nice, right? But somehow, it seems to become true. The more you repeat it, the less likely it is that you will do the thing you would like to. Now try putting the words '*I am having the thought that (…)*' in front of the statement, so it becomes '*I am having the thought that I am too old to (…)*'. Try closing your eyes and repeating this a couple of times. Does it feel any different? I have tried this with many people, and most find that it distances them from the ANT. After all, the ANT is just a thought, and thoughts are not necessarily facts or truths. They just randomly pop in and out of our heads. They are made up from things we have heard in our social lives, inner interpretations and the many biases hardwired into us. Do we really want to believe in them? In ACT terms, we allow ourselves to defuse the thoughts by not identifying with them or letting them become true.

This ability to step back and observe our thoughts can help us navigate the ageing process. It is a way to cope with the various self-limiting thoughts that have gotten stuck in our heads over many years of living, and instead turn our focus to the things that matter to us.

Jackie was 75 when she joined one of my mindfulness courses. She had diligently tried her best to cope with health and weight challenges, and she kept herself mentally engaged with online courses, one of which was on mindfulness. Although she was very sceptical about mindfulness at first, she quickly warmed up to it. She said it helped her accept that there are things she can no longer do, and that she did not have to just sit alone, shutting herself away from the world. Jackie lives alone after her husband's passing. She is by nature a very active, open-minded, knowledge-seeking and adventurous woman, but she had found it difficult to do things on her own. She wanted to travel and explore various cities but was held back by thoughts of being too old and travelling being too challenging for her to do by herself. Mindfulness made her aware of those self-limiting ANTs. She said it gave her a certain control over her thoughts and emotions, which gave her the courage and confidence to give travelling a go. At the end of the course, Jackie told me that she would go and visit some of the cities close by, just for a few days to start with. Jackie's story is an inspiring example of spotting our ANTs and curiously investigating and defusing them in order to move towards the things that give us pleasure. Like Jackie, we can broaden our perspective and listen to not only our critical inner voice but also our dreams and hopes. We will discuss having a broad perspective in Chapter 9.

START TO PRACTISE: CHOICE OF MINDSET

In the third part of the book, we investigate the last of the four phases of the ageing upwards framework: *embrace it!* The acronym eMBrACe reflects the elements of the framework, and in this chapter, we looked at 'M' for Mindset. The main points are:

- Our mindset matters for our well-being and our physical health.

- Most of the time, ageing isn't the problem; rather, it is the way we think about ageing.

- It is possible to reframe ageing by, for instance, replacing the narrative of decline with one of change and transition.

- *Socioemotional selectivity theory* states that due to the perception of time, older people become more selective in what we deem important and start to notice the positive more than the negative.

- Although we do not have control over our thoughts, we can control our attention and our response to what we hear.

- It is possible to turn innate and habitual tendencies to think *automatic negative thoughts* (ANTs) into tendencies to think *positive enhancing thoughts* (PETs).

- It is possible to *defuse* difficult thoughts.

The two guided meditations *Awareness of thoughts* and *Reframing ageing* will help you practise the skills in this chapter. To access the audio files, scan this QR code or go to www.ageingupwards.com.

CHAPTER 9

BROADEN YOUR PERSPECTIVE

IF YOU CAN'T BEAT THEM, JOIN THEM

Don't you sometimes wish that there was a switch at the back of our heads that could turn off our minds and stop all those disturbing and stressful thoughts? I did! I had read that with mindfulness I could learn to 'silence the mind', which is what made me sign up to my first five-day silent mindfulness beginner's retreat. However, I soon found out that when you sit down with the intention to stop thinking, the mind gets very active. A never-ending flow of thoughts flooded my mind while I tried to focus on my breath. *'Am I doing it right? I wish that man would stop breathing so loud. Why can't I just stop thinking? I suck at this. How long have I been sitting? What is for dinner?'* My body complained too. Sitting still on a cushion started to hurt my back, and my mind jumped at this opportunity to keep chatting: *'Why does my back hurt so much? Stop thinking about your back. Focus on your breath. But my back hurts. How can I make it go away? I suck at this!'*

I wasn't the only one who struggled, and on the second evening, our teacher gave us the golden nuggets that have shaped my life ever since. She said that when you experience difficulties in life, you have two ways to cope with them. You can change the situation, or you can change your attitude to the situation. So, first, I tried to change the situation. I changed the way I was sitting. I sat on a chair, or up against a wall. I propped myself up with cushions. I even tried to lie down, which made me fall asleep. None of it really worked. I moved on to option two, where I became conscious of my attitude. Under the guidance of my teacher, I explored the actual physical sensations that were happening in my body as well as how my mind reacted with old habitual patterns of resistance. I didn't know it, but I was going through the loop of noticing, noting and knowing, repeatedly gaining more and more awareness along the way. I went beyond the initial label of 'pain' and asked myself: *'How does it actually feel? Does the sensation in my back have a temperature, a colour, a texture? Does it move or is it still? What urges do I have when feeling this sensation? What else is happening right now? Can I maybe allow it to be here while I choose to focus on something else – my breath for instance?'* The pain didn't go away. My back continued to hurt throughout the retreat, but I figured out a way to allow the pain to be there without it completely taking over my mind. Like a radio channel, I could let the pain play in the background, zoom out and notice all the other things that were present in the moment, and deliberately choose where to place my attention and how to respond to what I found. I learnt that if we can't beat the unwanted thoughts, emotions or physical sensations, we can 'join' them and thereby stop them from hurting us further and adding secondary suffering to our experience, as we looked at in Chapter 5. The ability to accept is the subject of this chapter. We are going to investigate the 'Br' in eMBrACe, which stands for cultivating a Broad perspective. It helps our well-being to apply a broad perspective that allows pleasant, neutral and unpleasant experiences to be present.

eMBrACe

A BROAD PERSPECTIVE HELPS US ACCEPT

This chapter is really about 'acceptance', but this is a troublesome word and I have therefore chosen to refer instead to having a 'broad perspective'. For many, to accept something means to give in or give up. Some people also believe that in order to accept something, we need to like it, want it or approve of it. This is not what acceptance means in the tradition of mindfulness. I have learned that other phrases work better: 'dropping the struggle', 'making room', 'expanding', 'holding it gently/lightly/softly/kindly', 'breathing into it', 'letting it be/go', 'opening up' or, my preference, 'broadening ones perspective'. Senior mindfulness teacher Kathy Ward, who I have mentioned in earlier chapters, prefers to invite people to 'practise acceptance', to underline that it is a gradual process which might start with simple curiosity, moving through to mere tolerance and allowance before we might be able to let it be part of a wide field of awareness. In this wide field of awareness, we are able and willing to let the unpleasant sensations come and go, but we also notice the pleasant aspects of our moment-to-moment experience. We might even be able to find a hidden gift in the unpleasant, a lesson learned, a meaning, a calling or a purpose. Kathy points out that acceptance is not like a ladder that we progress along. '*It's more like a game of snakes and ladders*', she says. '*One time we might be able to look at something with curiosity, the next moment we may not have the capacity to even sneak a peek. Sometimes acceptance is simply not possible.*'

STOP STRIVING AND YOU WILL ACHIEVE

When people join my courses, most of them have a specific reason for doing so. They want to be happier, less stressed, less anxious, more efficient, more creative, more compassionate or generally just happier. But here is the thing: the more attached they are to their goal, the less likely they are to achieve it. I tell them this in the first class and encourage them to let go of all their hopes and goals and just see what happens. This does not sit well in most ears. It is not what they want to hear. They want to hear me promise them a certain return for their time and money. I get that. Luckily, I recently found some research to back me up. At the beginning of 2022, a team of researchers published the result of a study which evaluated what influence the intention for meditation has on the result. They found that those participants who meditated with the intention of managing difficult feelings or getting rid of stress or fear largely did not reach their goals, while those participants who meditated with no intention other than being open and accepting whatever thoughts and feelings arose reaped the commonly found benefits of meditation: less anxiety, less worry, less depression and better mindful awareness.[98] This is the very frustrating paradox of mindfulness. You need to stop striving if you want to achieve something. Well-being does not come to us through hard work and effort alone, but requires us to do something that most of us find much harder – letting go of our battles and inviting the challenges in with acceptance, curiosity and kindness.

OUR INTELLIGENCE WILL NOT SAVE US FROM PAIN

A very instinctual way to avoid pain is to try to solve our problems with our intellect. Our mind is a *problem-solving-machine*, which makes sense from an evolutionary point of view. If we are hungry, we think of ways to get food; if we are wet and cold, we find ways to build shelter. It is all about survival, and our minds will always try to find ways to avoid discomfort and pain. Therefore, when we are experiencing signs of ageing, our mind will try to find ways to get back to feeling better – aka when we were younger, fitter and stronger. I might tell myself: *'If I start doing puzzles, I might get my memory back.' 'If I take vitamin supplements, I might keep my immune system strong.' 'If I do yoga....' 'If I meditate....'*

Of course, a lot of the time, our minds are right. We should keep as fit and healthy as possible. But, on the other hand, we must move away from the illusion that we can fix everything. When it comes to painful thoughts and emotions, problem-solving solutions do not help. When you are in the mist of strong feelings, these will have no, or even the opposite, effect. Next time you feel angry, just try asking yourself: *'How can I get rid of this urge to yell at somebody?'* Or try asking yourself to get rid of the anxiety growing in your stomach when you are about to do a presentation or a speech. Rational thoughts will rarely help you in such situations. The thing is, whatever you focus your attention on gets bigger, even if the intention is to get rid of it. So, when you think about ways to avoid the anxiety, the anxiety will be in focus and, instead of dampening it, you will add secondary suffering. Sometimes, in order to solve our problems, we need to turn off the struggle switch, as I mentioned in Chapter 5, and just 'sit with it'.

What does that mean exactly? Imagine for a moment that you are out for a walk along the beach. You have taken your shoes off to enjoy the feeling of sand between your toes and the soft waves rolling over your feet. Suddenly, you find yourself surrounded by quicksand. Your natural reaction would be to try to get out. You would move your legs and arms wildly, knowing that if you don't get out of this, you will die. But as you probably know, the more you struggle in quicksand, the faster and deeper you will sink. You might also know that if you simply relax and spread your body out, you will float. Of course, this is not easy to do when every instinct in your body and mind is telling you to do the opposite.

You might not know what it is like to be stuck in quicksand, so let's take another example that you most likely have experienced at some point in your life: difficulty sleeping. Imagine that you are lying in your bed. Tiredness has taken over your body and mind, but even so you cannot fall asleep. Something important is happening the next day, so you keep checking the time, and your brain continues to inform you that you will now only get five hours of sleep before the alarm clock goes off. You lie in bed catastrophizing over how you will feel tomorrow, imagining yourself walking around like a zombie and not performing or enjoying the day as you would have liked. The more you think about it, the more awake you become and the harder it is to get to sleep. You are struggling the same way you would if you were in quicksand, and by doing so, you are digging yourself deeper and deeper into a situation you want to avoid.

The same principle applies to ageing. The more we try to avoid or fight it, the more it will make us suffer and take control of us. When I asked Carmen, one of the participants of the MBVA pilot course, if she thought mindfulness will help her as she grows older, she pointed out that it already helps her by letting her accept situations. She gave me an example of getting dressed, looking in the mirror and seeing an older body. Instead of *'being horrified by the sight'*, as she described it, she was able to say: *'Yeah, it is not the same as 20 years ago. No, it is not perfect. But it's OK. This is me now.'* She concluded: *'If I am able to accept my reality every time, every day, and not long for the past or be afraid of the future, of course it will help me grow older.'*

ACCEPT THE IMPERMANENCE OF LIFE

In order to avoid secondary suffering, we need to acknowledge the presence of dukkha, which I introduced in Chapter 2. The discomfort and discontentment of living is not limited to older people. To grasp this fully, it helped me to investigate the concept of *impermanence*. At the heart of secondary suffering is wanting things to be permanent when they are not. Impermanence is the cornerstone of Buddhist teachings, and it remains one of the main teachings of secular mindfulness. The fact that everything constantly changes and nothing lasts is beyond any religious ideology. All you have to do is spend some time in nature and it becomes very clear. Seasons come and go; plants and animals are born and die. I mentioned Zen master Tenkei Roshi in Chapters 5 and 7. He puts it like this: *'You are a work in progress. You are not a noun, but a verb. It is like the movies, where you see a person moving and it is very realistic. But when you look closer, you realize that it is only frames that are stuck together. It is the same in life. We are constantly dying and being reborn. Constantly changing. We have no fixed substance, yet we carry an energy that has never been born and will never die, and that connects us with everyone and everything throughout this whole universe. Realizing this makes it easier to appreciate the life allotted to us and age gracefully.'*

If we can truly understand impermanence and accept that it is impossible for us to grasp and hold on to anything, we can stop attempting to do so, and with that goes the secondary suffering. This is not easy. Of course, we all know that 'everything changes', but do we truly understand this? The 10-day Vipassana retreat helped me make the distinction between knowing it with my intellect and 'really' knowing it with my body and heart.

One of the main points behind the simple life at a Vipassana retreat, which I described earlier, is to restrain engagement with our senses and thoughts, as they distract our attention outward and lead to either attraction or aversion. If the food was too good, for instance, we would get distracted by fantasies of what kind of taste sensations we would experience during lunch. This would lead to thoughts of food, physical sensations of hunger and maybe emotions of impatience, frustration and anger at having to wait. As described earlier, we were instructed to notice and label everything that we experienced. 'Notice it, note it, know it and let it go' became a mantra to follow. It was exhausting, to be honest, and I was by no means a perfect student. My thoughts were often carried away to stories from the past or imagining the future. I would very often imagine myself lying in my comfortable, warm bed, and I admit to counting down the days, as if I were being kept against my will. But as I was descending into misery, I also discovered peace and insight. I started to find myself calmly noticing yet another source of frustration, accepting it as a passing event and then simply letting it go. This way, I started to truly experience impermanence. If my roommate decided to get up at midnight and shower, thereby waking me up during the few hours available for sleep, I could note it, label all the unpleasant emotions that passed through me and then let it go. My previous self would have stayed awake ruminating about how inconsiderate she was, and I would start problem-solving, looking for ways to stop her from doing it again, which would have been rather difficult since we were not allowed to communicate. By the end of the retreat, I was able to respond to our nightly encounters with acceptance. I also got better at coping with my fellow meditators, noisily drinking water, sniffling, coughing, sneezing, moving or even crying or laughing, without letting myself get disturbed. Or I could let inner diversions – like an itchy foot, a sore back or random thoughts – come and pass. Again and again, I noticed how everything just passed by, and I was able to simply surrender to this impermanence of life.

The Buddhist philosophies are backed by science. Numerous studies indicate that the more we choose to accept whatever happens to us, the lower levels of distress, anxiety and dissatisfaction we will experience.[99] One study found the same results for older individuals.[100]

Impermanence is usually seen as something negative. Most of us fear the loss of what we love and are attached to. However, once you come to terms with it, it is in fact very liberating to know that everything goes eventually and that life is a never-ending cycle of changes happening every second. Loss is painful, but it also brings freedom and opportunities.

BE A BIGGER CONTAINER

So how do we shift our minds to see impermanence as liberation? How do we practise acceptance? Let's imagine that you have spent the afternoon making yourself a tasty bowl of creamy tomato soup. As you sit down to eat, you accidentally drop a big spoonful of salt into the bowl. Your soup has suddenly become extremely salty. What do you do? If you are like most people, you will immediately swear and call yourself a lot of unpleasant things. Instead, I invite you to focus your attention on the size of the bowl of soup. Suppose it is the size of an espresso cup. It is tiny. What do you think a spoonful of salt would do to your lovely soup in such a small container? Ruin it, right? There is pretty much nothing else but salt in there. Now let's envision that the soup container is the size of one of those huge pots they use in industrial kitchens. That is a lot of soup. What would a spoonful of salt do to that amount of soup? It would probably still affect it, and you would probably rather this hadn't happened, but if you take a moment to really taste the soup, there would still be sweet flavours of tomato left and you would still feel the creaminess in your mouth. The taste of the unpleasantness would be diluted.

My point is that we can open up to the unpleasantness of life by becoming bigger containers ourselves. Since life consists of pleasant, unpleasant and neutral sensations constantly coming and going, it is pretty much impossible to be in a moment without there being a pleasant sensation present. We just need to notice it. All we must do when things are difficult is sit down and ask ourselves: '*What else is here right now?*' It is so easy to place all our attention on the salt alone and let it ruin everything else, but the alternative is straightforward. What other flavours can you taste in this moment?

So, when you notice yourself getting caught up in thoughts about all the things that you can no longer do, ask yourself: '*What else is here?*' It might be something small in the present moment – the sound of birds, the softness of a blanket or the smell of coffee. The expression 'to broaden ones perspective' makes acceptance practical and understandable, as it encourages us to make space inside ourselves. To dilute and accept an unpleasant sensation, we need to take a moment to open up and place it in a bigger container with all the other little things that are present right now and just watch them all come and go. Luckily, pleasant or neutral things are always at our disposal. We just need to notice them.

This approach to acceptance underpins that we do not need to like or want something in order to accept it. To broaden our perspective means that we acknowledge things are the way they are. It doesn't mean that we give up hope. Nor do we stop working towards achieving something. I am not advocating that you stop trying to create a better life. If you have chronic pain or illness, I am not telling you to resign yourself to a life of pain and suffering. I don't want you to become a doormat for unkind and hurtful people either. Mindful acceptance is about opening up to what is in this very moment. Right now! Sit with whatever thoughts, emotions and physical sensations are present. Notice, note and know them, and then find a way to embrace them. This means changing them if you can, or changing your perception of them if you can't.

BROAD PERSPECTIVE ON PAIN, ILLNESS AND DEATH

To embrace life is easier said than done, especially when it comes to losing loved ones or experiencing pain, illness and decline. How can we accept all the hardships of life? If we are lucky enough to grow old, we will probably get plenty of opportunities to practise. It has been found that 72% of people over 85 experience chronic pain in some form,[101] with the back, legs, knees and hip joints being the most common places where older individuals experience pain.[102] Living with pain can very easily become like salt in an espresso cup. It takes over people's lives completely. Understandably, most people will try every way possible to get rid of the pain, or at least ease it. Their lives become centred around their pain, and they start to identify strongly with it. It becomes who they are. They don't *have* an illness or disability; they *are* their illness or disability.

An interesting recent study from the University of California-San Diego School of Medicine investigated how identifying with our pain influences our experience of it. The study compared brain scans of two groups of people attending two sessions in which painful heat was applied to their legs. One group received four 20-minute meditation classes in between these sessions and were asked to meditate during the pain; the other group listened to an audiobook during their four class times, and were told to close their eyes during the sessions when heat was applied. The meditating group reported less pain intensity in the second session, after the classes, and the brain scans from the two groups gave a clue as to why: the meditating group had a less active *default mode network* (DMN). The DMN refers to an interconnected group of brain structures, which become spontaneously active when a person is engaged in introspective activities such as daydreaming or contemplating the past or future. It is also associated with thoughts about oneself. It seemed like the less an individual associated themselves with the pain sensations, the less pain they felt. According to the senior researcher on the study, Fadel Zeidan, PhD: 'One of the central tenets of mindfulness is the principle that you are not your experiences. You train yourself to experience thoughts and sensations without attaching your ego or sense of self to them, and we're now finally seeing how this plays out in the brain during the experience of acute pain.'[103]

The experienced Vipassana practitioner Stephen Thomas, who we met in Chapter 4, says that his consistent meditation practice has enabled him to detach from any kind of pain or illness and instead approach them with calm distance and curiosity: '*So, I feel pain. This is interesting. Let me observe. Not only will I enjoy the sensation of my sickness, I don't think it will kill me as quickly, because I will not waste energy. If I spend all my gas on worrying about it, I can't heal. If I observe with curiosity and self-compassion, then I can heal.*' Stephen actually said that he wants to '*enjoy*' his sickness. Is that really possible? Stephen gives an example from when he was one of the first people to catch COVID-19. He had serious trouble breathing, and at the time there was very little medical assistance to be had and a shortage of ventilators. He managed to not let anxiety take control of him. He observed that when he laid down in bed, he felt like his lungs were collapsing. So, for three nights he sat up to sleep, calmly observing his breathing, breathing deeply, in and out, to get as much air into his lungs as possible. His major objective was to observe how it felt to have difficulties breathing. He is convinced that his life would have been at stake if he hadn't responded in this way. *'Most people, when they experience something unusual, they get anxious. Why not approach something unusual by saying "Ah! So, this is what it's like to not breathe. Oh, wonderful! So, this is what it feels like to fill my lungs with air, even when I feel like my lungs are collapsing!" Of course, my family and a hospital was close by and I was ready to call them, if needed.'* I find it amazing that Stephen was able to stop all secondary suffering, the worries and anxious thoughts, in such a serious and highly emotional situation. Let me be clear, I am not suggesting meditation as an alternative to medical care for a deadly virus. Stephen was able to cope with a situation that could not be treated medically by flowing with it.

My Vipassana teacher Mike Helmle, who we met in Chapters 2 and 5, describes a similar ability, while observing his mother dying, to detach from his emotions and worries. Mike's mother was diagnosed with cancer and died within two and a half months. He describes how, during those months, he witnessed her falling apart. Although it was a very difficult time for him, his meditation practice enabled him to see the decline for what it was, beyond the thoughts of *'look at my poor mum suffering'*. Mike described his mother's process of dying as having a *'sense of beauty'*, as he watched her make peace with her life. *'When people are faced with their own death, it is forcing them into the present moment. It is forcing them to let go of everything that is not important in their lives. All of a sudden, the veil of ignorance and illusions start to drop'*, he explains. *'People on their deathbed start to realize what is important. They start to regret things and apologize and make amends for the things they have done'*. Mike witnessed his mother break down to her core humanity when all else was stripped away. She died in his arms, where he held her without tears. *'It was a beautiful experience, because I knew what she was going through was just an experience as any other in this impermanent world.'*

This final realization of what it means to be human and what is truly important is what we try to achieve when we meditate. Mike believes it gives us the upper hand so that we don't come completely unprepared for the end of our time. Meditation allows us at an early stage to accept reality as it is, knowing that nothing is here to stay. We don't need to wait until death forces us to see this. If we can recognize and open up to this while we are still living, it will prepare us to make peace with death.

To broaden our perspective and invite and feel the unpleasant parts of life requires a lot of courage. It also helps tremendously if we are able to meet it with an affectionate mindset, which is the focus of Chapter 10.

START TO PRACTISE: BROAD PERSPECTIVE

In this chapter, we continued to investigate the last of the four phases of the ageing upwards framework: *embrace it!* In this chapter, we looked at the 'Br' – cultivating a Broad perspective – in the eMBrACe acronym. The chapter's main points are:

- We add more pain and suffering to ourselves when we resist difficulties.

- Instead, we can practice acceptance by allowing difficult sensations to be present.

- If we open up to the pleasant, unpleasant and neutral sensations in the moment, we dilute the unpleasant.

- If we can truly understand that everything in the world is impermanent and that it is impossible for us to grasp and hold on to anything, we can avoid a lot of self-created suffering.

- Through meditation, we can train ourselves to experience difficult thoughts and pain without attaching our sense of self to them. This will not only reduce the level of physical pain, but also help us meet illness and death with curiosity, acceptance and self-compassion.

The two guided meditations *Exploring thoughts, emotions and physical sensations* **and** *Exploring pleasant, neutral and unpleasant sensations* **will help you practice the skills in this chapter.** To access the audio files, scan this QR code or go to www.ageingupwards.com.

CHAPTER 10

PRACTISE AFFECTION FOR YOUR SELF AND OTHERS

WE ARE SOCIAL BEINGS

I recently got a new running watch. As the watch registered all the details about my habits and bodily workings, it kept adjusting what it calls my 'fitness age'. It felt like I had found a time machine. Every time I went for a run, I was rewarded with the message 'Congratulations! Your fitness age has decreased', which made me feel even younger. I wondered if I could get to the age of 20 if I just kept running. Eventually it stopped, of course, and so did the regular burst of dopamine I got as a reward. This made me reflect on the connection between the body and mind, the many ways we can measure our age and what that knowledge does to our well-being. As a fun exercise for myself, I decided to take notice of the situations in which I feel full of vitality, and I noticed this was not related so much to exercise as to social relationships. I often find myself being tired after a day of work and reluctant to go out for the evening. However, I noticed that when I do go out, my energy levels lift, and I feel happy and vitalized in the moment. Social interaction and connections make me feel younger. Although it is not (yet) possible to measure our 'social age' like we can measure our fitness age, science is very clear that our health and well-being depend on the company of others. A study found that the fewer social ties we have, the higher our risk of heart disease, cancer or impaired immune function. Loneliness has been associated with a higher level of the stress hormone cortisol, which raises the risk of cardiovascular disease.[104] We are also worse at recovering from health problems when we lack social relationships.[105] A review of 148 studies found that people with stronger social relationships had a 50% increased likelihood of survival than those with weaker social relationships.[106]

In this chapter, we will look at how to improve our well-being and vitality by mitigating loneliness and improving relationships. We are going to cultivate the 'A' for Affection in the acronym eMBrACe, as a mindset of affection, love, compassion and common humanity benefits our own lives and those of the people around us.

A CHOICE BETWEEN THE FORCES WITHIN US

Human beings are hardwired to love and bond with each other. Fossils tell us that love evolved hundreds of millions of years ago as a way for our mammalian ancestors to survive.[107]

If our ancestors had not been able to care and love, they wouldn't have looked after each other, and we would not be here today. Just think about the inordinate amount of care human infants require, and our unusually long maturation period. Although words like 'love', 'compassion' and 'affection' can make us feel uncomfortable and the ability to feel and cultivate them in others is often dismissed as *soft skills*, they are in reality hardcore. Our bodies and minds are wired in many ways to encourage giving and seeking kindness and compassion. Our endocrine system, for instance, rewards us with pleasant hormones whenever we feel protected and wanted by other human beings.[108]

The challenge is that there are other competing innate forces within us. Aggression, violence, rage, selfishness and anger serve the same evolutionary purpose of keeping us safe. Morals and rules can tame and inhibit these dark, aggressive forces in civilized societies to a certain degree, but at the same time our highly competitive culture enforces them. In the end, it is up to each one of us to decide which forces within us we choose to nurture.

EXPAND YOUR IN-GROUPS

In 1979, French social psychologist Henri Tajfel came up with *social identity theory*,[109] which gives us an explanation for why we feel compassion towards some people and aggression towards others. Based on research and observation inside and outside the laboratory, he noted that the way a person behaves and their sense of identity are based on what groups they believe themselves to be part of. We get our identity from self-defined in- and out-groups. For instance, some of the categories of people I consider as my in-groups are females,

Europeans, middle-aged people, mothers, entrepreneurs, meditators and, recently, authors. Some of my out-groups would be males, young people and meat eaters. Tajfel said that we are wired to exaggerate all the negative ways we are different from our out-groups and all the positive qualities we share with our in-groups. A common source of identification is gender. Personally, I often find myself identifying with an in-group of 'females' as I feel like they somehow 'get me'. But do they really? All 3.9 billion of them?[110] The same questions could be asked about age. Do I really have more in common with all the people of my own age than with people who are younger or older than me? But we define ourselves according to random in-groups all the time. We judge and stereotype based on gender, religion, race, beliefs, skin colour, career choice, place of origin, the brand of washing powder we use – you name it! It gives us a sense of belonging, but the downside is racism, sexism, ageism and all the other isms of the world.

When we combine our tendency to split the world into 'them' and 'us' with our two inner forces of aggression and compassion, we get a dangerous cocktail. Not just for world peace but for the well-being of each one of us. What happens is that we allow our innate forces of aggression to be directed towards our out-groups and our feelings and actions of compassion, towards our in-groups. From an evolutionary point of view, it makes perfect sense – protect the genes in your in-group against the threatening forces from the outside. From a well-being perspective, it is a very bad strategy. First, we run a high risk of getting very lonely and isolated if we limit our social relations to like-minded people, especially when we get older and the members of our chosen in-groups start to die. Second, although the adrenalin from aggression might feel good in the moment, it is not a feeling that will make us happy in the long term. Compassion, on the other hand, will; there has been a clear association found between feeling compassion and well-being.[111]

The good news is that once we become aware of our hardwiring through practising the notice, note and know loop, we can find ways to counteract it. The answer is simple. We can expand our in-groups. Let there be more of 'us' than 'them'. Not by getting rid of our out-groups, of course, but by mentally enlarging our in-groups to include more people. If we work hard at it, it might even be possible to make the whole world our in-group. We could start to meet the world with an attitude that says we are all alike as human beings, instead of exaggerating the things that set us apart.

I talk from experience. During the many meditations at my Vipassana retreat, I cultivated a lot of compassion, kindness and affection. After 10 days, my heart was so full of it that I experienced a completely different journey home than I had anticipated. Going on a cheap airline with stressed employees and fellow travellers can be a rather stressful experience, especially during a pandemic, but I found myself extremely calm. I had strong feelings of compassion and the urge to go and hug everyone. The crying children, the tired parents, the person who slowed us all down by bringing nail clippers and scissors in her purse, the loud businesswoman talking on her phone, the man eating eggs with a strong smell – I saw them all as belonging to my group of fellow human beings, each with feelings, challenges, faults and talents. It was amazing. Unfortunately, it didn't last. The 'Vipassana effect' wore off after a while. I will admit that I occasionally can be found cursing over people cutting in front of me in queues and secretly assigning them to some random out-group of mine. The retreat did, however, give me an insight into how it is possible to nurture those nicer qualities within me and how good it made me feel to meet the world with such an attitude. As we saw in Chapter 6, compassion is a highly predictive trait for well-being.

AFFECTION FOR OTHERS

Professor Barbara Fredrickson's book *Love 2.0* has a brilliant message based on solid scientific evidence: love is something we can become better at through practice.[112] 'Love' is a big word and might put some people off. However, Fredrickson is not talking about romantic love here, but rather loving connection. She says that it is possible to strengthen our capacity for love by sitting in the safety of our homes and practising certain meditations. Or we can go out and explore what she calls 'micro-moments of connection'. These can be experienced with any person (or even an animal) by just allowing ourselves to connect with them for brief moments. We don't have to know the person. They can be a total stranger. All it takes is a moment of eye contact, a short conversation about the weather, a smile – anything that creates a moment of connection between you and them.

You might wonder what it means to sit in the safety of our homes and practise compassion. It is a bit like when professional athletes visualize their performance before a competition. By imagining their movements, they are stimulating the same brain regions as they would if physically performing that same action. Just as athletes can condition their brains for successful outcomes, we can condition our brains and bodies for feeling love and compassion. *Loving kindness meditation* is a kind of kindness visualization. It is a secular version of an old Buddhist practice known as *mettā*, where the meditator systematically sits and generates kindness and compassion for themselves and others. It is inherent in any mindfulness course. The meditation usually invites us to send love and kindness to ourselves, a good friend, a neutral person and a person we have difficulty with, and finally we grow our circle of imagined people in the mind, spreading love and kindness to the whole world, across all our differences.

Loving kindness meditation can leave you in an amazing state fulfilled by peace and love, but it can also be a very frustrating experience. In my courses, I will always have a few participants who experience strong feelings of self-hate or sadness because they are not able to generate the feelings of loving kindness that are encouraged. Instead, their inner critical voice tells them that they are not worthy of kindness or affection. It takes an enormous amount of compassion and courage to cultivate compassion towards ourselves. All we can do is take small steps.

AFFECTION FOR YOUR SELF

Here is an exercise for you. Take a piece of paper and write down five words that describe you as a person. Then think of a good friend and write down five words that describe your friend. Now compare the two lists and see if there is an equal amount of positive and negative words. If you are anything like the average person, you will find that the words you have used to describe yourself are more on the negative side than the qualities you chose for your friend. We are typically not very nice to ourselves. In the last chapter, I suggested you get to know your ANTs. Do ANTs come up when you think about your best friend? Most of us do not judge our friends in the negative way we judge ourselves. Why? Because our caveman brain is working hard at keeping us safe, of course. By focusing on our own negative traits, we can learn from our mistakes and prevent ourselves from getting into embarrassing situations that might risk social exclusion or reduce our chances of getting a partner and making sure our genes go into the next gene pool. On the other hand, we need to stay on good terms with our friends to benefit from the safety of belonging to a group. Once again, the caveman wiring of our brain is not good for our well-being.

The antidote is being affectionate towards ourselves. Turn the innate compassionate forces within you 180 degrees around and treat yourself with kindness. There are strong associations between self-compassion and well-being among older individuals[113] and for all age groups.[114] Kristin Neff, a professor of educational psychology at the University of Texas at Austin, is a pioneer on self-compassion. She defines self-compassion as consisting of three things:

- **Mindfulness:** noticing and knowing judgements in order to change them;
- **Self-kindness:** meeting challenges with warmth and understanding;
- **Common humanity:** recognizing that suffering is part of being human and that it is OK to not be OK from time to time.

The following is an example of meeting difficulties with self-compassion: '*Hmm… today I noticed that I had a moment of confusion. That is OK; it is normal from time to time. I notice that my mind goes off on all sorts of worries about what this moment of confusion might mean or lead to. Is this helping me live the life I want to live? No! What can I do right now to be kind to myself instead of wasting my time worrying? I think I need to call my friend and go for a walk with her.'* Notice that this is not self-pity – there is no 'poor me' or 'why me?' This is not ignoring problems either; it is just stopping the secondary suffering from taking over and instead doing something that actively soothes the difficulties. Of course, if the incidents of confusion repeat, then it might be time to respond in a different way and call the doctor.

TAKE RESPONSIBILITY FOR LONELINESS

The ability to meet difficulties with acceptance and self-compassion can empower us to cope with one of the challenges that many older people face: loneliness. Loneliness among older individuals is widespread.[115] According to a recent advocacy brief from the World Health Organization (WHO) on social isolation and loneliness among older people, there is a large body of research indicating that social isolation and loneliness seriously impact physical and mental health, quality of life and longevity for older people. WHO also points out that loneliness imposes a heavy financial burden on society.[116]

Due to the seriousness of loneliness, a lot of interventions have been suggested and tried out to ease the problem. This is, of course, great, and a lot can be done on a cultural and societal level to mitigate the problem. However, it is the same as with ageism. We as older people cannot afford to sit and wait for society to save us. We need to be open to investigating how we are contributing to the problem and making sure we do whatever we can ourselves right now. So, what can we do?

First, we must acknowledge that loneliness is an emotion, a message from our body and mind that something is not right. An emotion urges us to fulfil a need, which in this case is social connection. Let's start with the easiest solution. Based on evidence, the absolute best way to beat loneliness, or any uncomfortable feeling of sadness and unhappiness for that matter, is to help, or give something to, other people. Giving makes us happy,[117] it is good for our health[118] and it promotes cooperation and social connection.[119] We can give anything, big or small. Even just giving a smile to someone makes you feel better. Remember Fredrickson's micro-moments of connection. When we talk about combatting loneliness, we might benefit from starting out small. If we just aim to become better at giving and receiving small acts of connection and kindness, they will grow over time and eventually our lives will be much more full of these.

There are plenty of other ways to improve our social connections. When I was studying for my master's degree in Vitality and Ageing, I interviewed an older gentleman about ways to combat loneliness. He said something very wise, along the lines of: *'Yes, of course, we all need to include older people in our lives. We need to invite them more, spend time with them, talk and listen to them. BUT, what is most important in order to combat loneliness is that the person who is invited makes sure they invite people back!'* For loneliness to end, there needs to be active engagement happening on both sides. And, yes, maybe the person that is invited to dinner is not able to shop and cook, but we can always find other ways to connect.

We can also help ourselves by proactively seeking and choosing the right company. What I experience every time I teach an eight-week mindfulness course in terms of support and bonding between the participants is a great example of this. Bonding can happen almost automatically if you put people together in a place where they feel safe and where they feel they have something in common. Like so many others, I started to teach online during the pandemic and, at first, I worried that the usual connection would not happen. But, it did! Very much so. Even though participants were sitting in different parts of the world, were of different nationality, skin colour and gender identity, and interacted via screens. The pandemic seemed to give them even more purpose to bond; it became the common enemy that the group could beat together. This innate ability and desire to connect – especially during adversity – is truly magical. We can avoid loneliness by continuing to find new groups to engage with and by expanding our existing in-groups to include more people. If we place ourselves in situations that matter to us and among people that have a common goal, we often find that connections, bonding and a sense of purpose and worth will flourish. This could be joining (or initiating) groups with an interest in sport, board games, books, knitting, vintage cars or drones. You name it! We do not need to limit our interest to something age related. And even if we are not able to leave our homes due to health or disability issues or because of geographical distance, there are many things happening online.

OK, so what if I am an introvert, lack social skills and my caveman brain fears rejection? This is where self-compassion can be very powerful. You could start in the safety of your own home with mindfully noticing, noting and knowing the resistance and uncomfortable feelings and meeting these with an attitude of curiosity through meditation. This seems worthwhile as studies have found that the effects of meditation in alleviating loneliness are promising.[120] Another component of self-compassion, according to Neff, is to remind ourselves of common humanity. So point out to yourself that it is perfectly normal to feel socially awkward and insecure. We all feel like that from time to time. While still at home, you could try the last component to meet or investigate the challenge with warmth and understanding. You could, for instance, examine your beliefs with self-kindness. Could you defuse from the ANT: '*I am lacking social skills*'? And maybe turn it into a PET: '*I am brave because I am practising being social despite my fears.*' When you are ready, you can start to practise in the real world, taking small steps and noticing what works and what doesn't, returning to the safety of your meditation mat when needed. You will probably need to go through the process many times. The ability to interact is a skill we can all get better at, but we need to be brave enough to step out of autopilot and curiously investigate how we engage with others and ourselves. Maybe you notice that you judge people too harshly or reject them as not part of your in-group, thereby missing out on potential friendships? Or you might find that others avoid you because you talk too much about yourself and take little interest in their lives? Or perhaps you judge yourself too harshly and have a head full of ANTs that are stopping you from engaging, making yourself invisible or hard to approach?

My description of how to overcome social fear and lack of skills might sound as if it is an easy thing to do. It is not. Far from it! It is a cruel reality that we are genetically wired to need connection with other people, yet social interaction is something we must learn by engaging in life. I have included the previous paragraph to illustrate that even though you might be filled with thoughts of yourself as an 'introvert', a 'loner' or 'socially awkward', these are all just thoughts (ANTs) that can be reframed. They are inner pathways that can be redirected, and skills can be practised to help you move on. If the last paragraph speaks to you, please remember that to confront thoughts like these takes a lot of courage and a lot of self-compassion, so well done!! You are a pioneer when it comes to combatting loneliness from within. But please reach out to a friend, a therapist or a mindfulness coach if you need help.

For many of the participants on my MBVA course, learning about and practising self-compassion was a great help. They all mentioned it as one of the main benefits they took away from the course and predicted that it would be a skill that allows them to cope with the challenges that come with age. To be able to meet oneself as a friend gives us power and strength. If we want our friends to succeed at something, we encourage them and we give them love and comfort when they fail or suffer, because we know that this is what they need to get back up again. Aggression and criticism do not help us get though hardships, and it doesn't encourage us to learn and move on either. What kind of children would we raise if we met their failed attempts to walk, speak or eat with criticism? The same goes for us. Self-criticism leaves us powerless and distraught, whereas self-love can empower us and help us see when we are stuck with unhealthy beliefs and in unhealthy patterns. Love, kindness and compassion are needed for us to be able to accept and adapt to the harsh realities of life and age.

In Chapters 8–10, we have looked at cultivating a mindset that allows us to embrace the challenges of life. Most of our effort so far has relied on continually practising our inner mindfulness muscles. Sometimes, it is enough to change our inner mindset in order to change. At other times, however, we need to make more drastic changes in the way we live life. The last chapter will take a more external focus and explore ways of adapting to life as it changes.

START TO PRACTISE: AFFECTION FOR SELF AND OTHERS

In this chapter, we continued to investigate the last of the four phases of the ageing upwards framework: *embrace it!* We looked at cultivating an Affectionate mindset (the 'A' in eMBrACe) towards ourselves and others. The main points are:

- It is important for our well-being to have social relationships.

- Words like 'love', 'compassion' and 'affection' are often dismissed as *soft skills* – in reality, these feelings are hardcore and we wouldn't survive without them.

- We have two forces within us: kindness and compassion for the people close to us and aggression towards the people we perceive as threats. It is up to us which forces we cultivate.

- *Social identity theory* explains how we divide people into in- and out-groups. A way to create thriving lives is to expand our in-groups and focus on how we are alike instead of how we are different.

- It is possible to strengthen our capacity for love by practising certain meditations and cultivating micro-moments of connection.

- Self-compassion is a skill we can become better at.

- Loneliness is widespread among older individuals, but we can do a lot ourselves to mitigate it.

The two guided meditations *Meeting challenges with self-affection* **and** *Loving kindness meditation (mettā)* **will help you practise the skills in this chapter.** To access the audio files, scan this QR code or go to www.ageingupwards.com.

CHAPTER 11

COMMIT TO ACTIVELY ADAPTING

Whenever I do a talk or workshop on mindfulness in corporations, there will often be a listener who gets impatient and says something along the lines of: *'But we are not going to change anything by closing our eyes and sitting on a mat. Let's get on with business and DO something!'* You might feel the same and wonder how one can possibly create a better life by sitting still. The answer is that of course we can't – not alone. It is time to add the last element of the acronym eMBrACe: 'C', which stands for Committing to actively adapting to new contexts. I refer here to Chapter 2, where I introduced you to functional contextualism and gave the example of an old knife which still had a variety of purposes despite its blade being dull. I talked about how we need to see our lives in a flow of continually changing contexts and find creative and flexible ways to adjust and fit into them. We have already done the groundwork and are mentally well prepared to do so by continually going through the loop in the ageing upwards framework. Now we need to act.

eMBrACe

STRATEGIES TO FIND PURPOSE WITHIN NEW CONTEXTS

Staying with the metaphor of the dull knife, there are ways we can adjust the purpose of the knife to fit with its new context. We need to 'select' its new purpose, 'optimize' it for that purpose and maybe find a way to 'compensate' for the things it can no longer do. I get these three terms from the *selection, optimization and compensation* (SOC) model, which was developed by the psychologists Paul and Margaret Baltes. It consists of these three self-regulatory strategies for adaptation:[121]

- **Selection** focuses on deciding where to focus one's resources and setting goals in a certain domain, while optimization and compensation focus on ways to achieve those goals.
- **Optimization** means maximizing gains by developing one's potential in terms of improving strengths and abilities.
- **Compensation** refers to minimizing losses by looking for alternative ways to pursue goals. This could be achieved by acquiring new resources or by applying unused internal or external resources.

Studies have shown positive results from use of the SOC model as a strategy to improve well-being among older individuals, both in selecting and optimizing their abilities and in compensating for declines and losses. It has been found to improve satisfaction with ageing, increase positive emotions, decrease loneliness, and improve subjective physical health and happiness.[122] In the following, I have been inspired by these three practical ways to bring our mindfulness practice into actions.

SELECT YOUR PRIORITIES WISELY BY PAUSING

As we saw in Chapter 7, it is important for our well-being to choose a purpose and adjust it to our abilities. We also need to select where to place our focus, as we saw in Chapter 8. This has nothing to do with our age. We make selections throughout our lives. Our time and resources are limited, and we cannot attend to everything. A lot of the time we make our selections unconsciously, attending to the things that seem most urgent or simply because somebody is screaming the loudest. I have found that a lot of the people who participate in my MBSR courses try to do everything (often at the same time) and let others around them or deadlines dictate what they should use their scarce resources on. Mindfulness helps them pause and become aware of their priorities. If you are retired, deadlines might not be a big issue anymore, but you will still find that others will try to decide for you where you should focus your attention. This could be well-meaning families or doctors thinking you should prioritize safety over adventure, or it could be your own unconscious beliefs about how retirees *ought* to spend their lives.

Pausing allows you to prioritize wisely. Vipassana practitioner Stephen Thomas, who we met in Chapter 4 and again in Chapter 9, refers to *'the power of non-doing'* and *'the secret of stopping'* as benefits of meditating. Similarly, the participants who took part in the MBVA pilot course pointed out afterwards that the new habit of taking pauses, stepping back and observing helped them immensely to reset and meet whatever life brings with awareness, openness, acceptance and self-compassion. One participant of the MBVA course puts it like this: *'All the thoughts sometimes build up and sometimes you just go in a circle. So, you can break and step away. That is what I have learnt and that is what I find very useful with mindfulness. My mind gets another set-up. I am stepping out of the circle so I can see everything at a distance.'*

Pauses can be just one minute, 40 minutes or days, depending on your situation and the urgency for your decision. In urgent matters, it helps if you have regularly practised the loop of the ageing upwards framework, as you will be much better equipped to do the same in stressful and challenging circumstances. If, on the other hand, you are in the habit of resisting and ignoring unpleasant thoughts and emotions, you are not going to be very well prepared to respond mindfully to, let's say, receiving difficult news of a serious medical diagnosis.

Pausing has another great benefit. By taking the time to step back and just breathe or notice the feeling of your feet on the floor, you will naturally let your nervous system calm down. You will go from the stress-induced fight/flight/ freeze sympathetic nervous system into the calm rest/digest/ connect parasympathetic system. This means that your body and mind no longer think that you are in immediate danger, and consequently you are less likely to make a hasty decision that is solely focused on your survival.

SET FLEXIBLE GOALS

Not only do we need to be flexible when we choose our focus and purpose, but the goals we set for ourselves also need to be. We set goals throughout our lives, and when we are young, we expect to achieve them if we just work hard enough. When we get older, there will be a lot of new and unpredictable factors relating to our capabilities, and we will need to be a bit more open to adjusting our goals along the way. It also helps to expand our understanding of what constitutes a goal. Most people believe goals are set in order to grow or gain in one way or another. One study found that younger adults are indeed motivated to aspire to growth and gains, but it is different for older people. The thing that motivated older people in the study was preserving what they already had.[123] A goal is not necessarily a destination, like a mountain peak we climb towards. It does not have to be something we either succeed in or fail at. It can also be a process that we keep working towards – like preservation. Some days we might be closer to our goal than others, but we might never be able to say that we have achieved it 100%. That doesn't mean that it is not a valid goal or that we have failed to attain it.

At 78, Herma-Jozé Blaauwgeers, who we met in Chapters 7 and 8, knows the importance of setting oneself definite but flexible goals in life. *'Yes, my body gives me limitations, but they are not of the nature that I cannot continue living my life. It is just a different life. I have a talk to my body every day. I say: "It is your job to be healthy and these are all the issues I would like to work on." I decide on a date and then I work towards it.'* But on the not-so-good days, she will say: *'So today I cannot…. What else can I do? And sometimes just hugging the couch is the perfect thing for the day.'*

A question that often pops up is that if we no longer need to strive and achieve, why should we continue to set ourselves goals? Aren't goals just for younger people to help them build careers and families? Nothing could be further from the truth. Goal selection and goal pursuit are important for both physical and mental health no matter our age, as there is a strong correlation between the pursuit of goals and well-being.[124] First, it is not whether you achieve your goals that makes you happy, but simply that you have them. The identity around having goals, the sense of direction they bring and the small steps we make towards progress confirm our own agency and willpower, which generates hope and makes us feel good. Second, having goals motivates us to make changes and improve our lives. We all know how hard it is to create new habits like eating more vegetables or exercising more, or to let go of bad habits like smoking. Having goals can motivate us and help us stick to a plan for achieving or maintaining something that will give us a better life. This does not change with age.

Unfortunately, our age can limit our opportunities for growth due to stereotypical views of older people.[125] Whenever we make selections and set goals, we therefore need to find out whether something is truly stopping us or if ageism ANTs are at play, as we investigated in Chapter 8. Of course, a silver lining lies in society's diminishing expectations about what we ought to strive for as an older person. It can be a great sense of relief that the pressure to achieve is lessened, as it gives us more freedom to decide which goals we want to set for ourselves and how to get there.

ACHIEVE YOUR GOALS

Once we have wisely selected our priorities and goals, we need to activate internal or external resources to work towards the goal. We can activate old resources or acquire new ones. If the calcification of your shoulders stops you from doing yoga, for instance, as in the case of Rita in Chapter 1, and you decide to explore alternative ways to connect with your moving body, you will need to find ways to optimize how you can achieve this goal. Maybe you can activate an inner willpower or reconnect with your love of learning. Maybe you will plan for how, when and where you are going to try out tai chi, qigong or similar. Maybe you will find ways to nudge yourself into doing daily YouTube exercises, such as having a place in the living room set up permanently for this purpose. Or maybe you will seek support from a friend and arrange to go to lessons together. These are just a few ways to optimize the odds of reaching our goals.

It is crucial that we are flexible in the progression towards attaining our goals. Some days our bodies and/or cognitive abilities work better than others, and it is important that we eMBrACe these challenges (notice, note and know our experiences, choose a Mindset that is Broad and Affectionate and, finally, Commit to adapt accordingly). Failure to achieve our goals is not necessarily a failure in living a healthy ageing life – it can be the opposite. It can be a sign that we are succeeding in responding mindfully to life by pausing and listening to the signals our bodies and minds are sending us. If we practise mindfulness regularly, we will discover that the pleasure we feel when achieving a goal is very short, but an accepting, compassionate progress towards achieving or maintaining a goal can give us longer-lasting pleasures, satisfaction and insights. A healthy ageing life is about finding the balance between having the discipline to pursue goals that will improve our lives and being able to embrace the things that hinder us.

FIND A SENSE OF AGENCY

No matter what our goal is, we need to believe we can obtain it, or at least get closer to obtaining it. The positive psychologist Rick Snyder did pioneer work on hope. He said that two factors decide whether people are able to shape their futures: *willpower*, which is the person's will to shape their future, and *waypower*, which is the person's ability to set a pathway towards a desired future.[126] The higher we score on both, the more able we are to shape our future and tackle difficult challenges. There is a copious amount of books out there giving practical advice on how to improve our waypower to achieve our goals. I will not repeat any of that here, but will stick instead to willpower, as this has to do with our mental abilities and is, therefore, something that mindfulness can help us with.

Our willpower is highly dependent on having *self-efficacy*,[127] which is an individual's belief in their ability to influence life events. Nobody in their right mind will make an effort if they don't believe the hard work will pay off. Among older individuals, high self-efficacy has been associated with better overall health,[128] increased energy, better sleep and decreased pain and discomfort as well as overall satisfaction with life.[129] Unfortunately, studies have also found that we tend to lose a sense of agency, which is similar to self-efficacy, when we age.[130] [131] Various interventions have, therefore, been created and studied to find ways of enhancing people's belief in their ability to influence their lives.[132] Some of these have focused successfully on people's ability to connect mind and body,[133] and my own study of MBVA is one of them. One of the realizations that participants on my course came to after practising mindfulness was that although we cannot avoid decline in certain abilities, a mental flexibility gives us the agency to compensate by using our other faculties.

ACCEPTANCE AS A GATEWAY TO COMPENSATION

The last strategy for adaptation in the SOC model is compensation. This is no doubt the hardest way to adapt, as it requires us to accept our losses. I have met older people who would rather sit inside all day than get out and face the world on a disability scooter. You would think that senior-directed products like scooters, wheelchairs or stairlifts would be very popular, as they can help us compensate for the things we can no longer do and thereby allow us to continue living independent lives. This is not always the case, however, because by getting on a scooter, one must also accept having a disability, which might bring up a lot of uncomfortable thoughts about being dependent on others and being unable to contribute to society. Being forced to compensate is hard mentally. But what is the alternative? Usually, it will not be something that helps us live better lives. By not accepting and compensating for our loss, we end up creating a lot of secondary suffering for ourselves. Luckily, even when we can no longer change the situation, we can still change our relationship with it. As the holocaust survivor Viktor Frankl said: 'Everything can be taken from a man but one thing: the last of the human freedoms—to choose one's attitude in any given set of circumstances, to choose one's own way.'[134]

Let's take Sebastian. Sebastian grew up in the fresh, cool mountain air of Switzerland, and for his whole life he has enjoyed hiking in this environment. Around the age of 65, he started to have problems with his balance. He began to fall over and felt unsafe when hiking rough, uneven mountainous terrain. Sebastian started to have thoughts like: '*I have to hike the mountains – they are my passion, my refuge, they are a part of me.*' '*I will never be able to enjoy my life if I can no longer hike.*' These thoughts led to more judgmental views of his own limitations, self-blame and resistance. Compensatory behaviours were not an option and he got stuck in a downward spiral of negative thoughts, emotions and an unhealthy habit of distracting himself with computer games. Eventually, Sebastian's wife got sick of his dark moods and looked for ways to break the spiral. She understood that Sebastian was completely absorbed with the thought that there was no alternative to his way of hiking. So, on his behalf, she decided to explore new options. She booked a weekend away for them in the flatlands of the Netherlands, where they were living at the time. She did a lot of research and found some nice hikes on paved roads, which had the upside of going past cosy restaurants where they could enjoy lunch and have a nice rest to break up the hike. Sebastian loved it. It was not the hikes of Switzerland he would have preferred, but it was still better than sulking at home. He found a way to compensate and to reconnect with his joy of nature, his body and his wife. Sometimes we need a little help to see and try out alternatives.

I fully believe that if we practise the loop of the ageing upwards framework, we will be much better equipped to find ways to compensate, thereby avoiding secondary suffering. If Sebastian had had a mindfulness practice, he would have been paying attention to the ANTs and his unhealthy behaviour patterns. He would have been aware of the unpleasant consequences he created for himself and his wife, and he would have been able to meet this awareness with a broad perspective. This is backed up by research. Researchers who investigated successful application of the SOC model found a theme of acceptance. They noticed that participants who reported a higher level of acceptance of their health conditions were also better at adapting.[135]

COMMIT TO THE PRESENT MOMENT

Let me finish with a personal story. My grandmother owned a small forest with a small cottage in the middle of it. She didn't live there, as it was quite primitive, didn't have electricity and was far away from any neighbours. But she drove to the forest as often as she could. It was very much part of who she was and how she lived her life. It was the place where the family would gather for Easter celebrations or meet to cut down our Christmas trees. In between the family get-togethers, she would take care of the forest, chopping down trees and planting new ones. Her old friend Christian Ejnar joined her on the daily trips until his death at 95. She continued on her own, selecting, optimizing and compensating when needed as she aged. In time, she could do less and less, and she became more dependent on the help of others. She had to let go of the chainsaw and the family insisted on her carrying a mobile phone for her safety. Eventually, she was also dependent on others to drive her there. When she couldn't go, she found compensation in the small garden in the rowhouse in which she lived. When the end of my grandmother's life was near, I drove her to her beloved forest for a few hours. She couldn't get out of the car, so we just opened the doors and sat there in silence. My grandmother didn't know the word 'mindfulness', but she was very mindful when she was in her forest. It was a glorious spring day and the leaves on the beech trees were florescent green. There was life all around us – birds were singing, bees were busy collecting nectar, mosquitos were biting us. It was a magical experience and I think my grandmother at that moment, despite being at the end of her life, was fully alive and present. Of course, she would have preferred to have been out there working and walking the forest with full physical vigour, but she was able to compensate by simply being present.

Thriving lives spring from the moments. Each new moment contains elements to mourn and elements to enjoy. No matter your age right now, don't get stuck regretting the loss of your youth, and don't worry about growing older either. If you notice, note and know life as it comes and are willing to embrace it, you will always be able to find something to learn and appreciate in the moments. As 91-year-old Viggo Uttrup, who we met in Chapter 3, says:

> *The sun shines just as well for us old*
> *people as it does for the young ones.*

START TO PRACTISE: COMMITMENT TO ACTIVELY ADAPTING

In this chapter, we continued to investigate the last of the four phases of the ageing upwards framework: *embrace it!* In this chapter, we looked at the 'C' – which stands for Commit to actively adapt to new contexts – in the acronym eMBrACe. The chapter's key points are:

- The *selection, optimization and compensation* model suggests three strategies to adapt to life and ageing.

- Taking pauses to look inwards and reflect allows us to prioritize our resources wisely.

- There is a strong correlation between the pursuit of goals and well-being.

- A sense of agency is important in the attainment of goals. This can be enhanced by an ability to connect mind and body.

- To be forced to *compensate* due to a decline in abilities is difficult, but regular practice in going through the loop of the ageing upwards framework will allow us to compensate with acceptance.

The guided meditation *Ageing upwards* is a longer meditation guiding you to practise all the skills of the ageing upwards framework. To access the audio files, scan this QR code or go to www.ageingupwards.com. By practising this formal meditation on a regular basis, mindful awareness and habits will empower you to actively adapt to life as it unfolds.

EPILOGUE

Does it suck to age, as my old military colleague told me 20 years ago, and how do we embrace it? What is my conclusion now that the book is written? Let me answer it this way.

I recently came back from a long holiday to find my little garden had grown completely out of control. Plenty of sun, warmth and an automatic watering system had made it flourish. Both the wanted plants and the unwanted weeds had grown. Uninvited slugs had feasted on my expensive plants, and cats had used the soil as a toilet. This is what will happen to a garden if left unattended. Our minds are like gardens. If there is no deliberate attempt to cultivate certain growth over others, we may not like the outcome. There are strong natural and random forces at play, and we need to pay attention and respond to these if we want to shepherd them in a certain direction.

Likewise, our minds need wise cultivation if we want to live and age well. If you think it sucks to live, then it will also suck to grow old. There will no doubt be plenty of unpleasant challenges, but they do not have to outshine all the other things that are present in our lives. Life contains pleasure and pain, beauty and ugliness, aggression and compassion. What we feed will grow stronger. The power of the unwanted will diminish if we can embrace it with awareness, acceptance and affection. This is a life skill which requires practice. The best way to ensure a thriving ageing life is to look after yourself now, whatever you age might be. If you can cultivate healthy mindful mental habits now, you are setting yourself up for not only longevity but also a fulfilling, purposeful life. My conclusion and invitation is to embrace the suck of ageing by embracing life – all of it! This is how we live and age upwards.

ACKNOWLEDGEMENTS

I wish to thank all the wise people who have inspired me and, in some cases, allowed me to interview them. This includes (but is not limited to) Vipassana teacher Mike Helmle, my mentor and senior mindfulness teacher Kathy Ward, former priest and hospice volunteer Viggo Uttrup, experienced Vipassana practitioner Stephen Thomas, coach Herma-Joze Blaauwgeers, abbot and Zen master Tenkei Coppens Roshi, Professor of Medicine of Old Age at the University of Copenhagen Rudi Westendorp, teachers and fellow students at the Master of Vitality and Ageing at Leiden University, my supervisors Professor David van Bodegom and Frank Schalkwijk at Leyden Academy on Vitality and Ageing, Brenda Childers, Courtney Smith van Rij, Jacqui Fairbrass and all the people who I have taught mindfulness to and who in return have taught me so much about life. Also thank you to the fabulous Alison Jones and her team at Practical Inspiration Publishing and my *street team* who have helped me navigate this new world of writing, publishing and promoting a book.

Most of all, I wish to thank Steve for all his support. We still don´t know where in the world we will end up, but no matter where and what will happen to us, I know there is no one else I would rather grow old with than you.

LIST OF GUIDED MEDITATIONS

The following recorded guided meditations are available for download at www.ageingupwards.com.

PRACTISE *NOTICE IT!*

 Skills introduced in Chapter 3:
- Notice it
- Playing with my attention

PRACTISE *NOTE IT!*

 Skills introduced in Chapter 4:
- Note it – labelling our experiences
- Body scan
- Mindful movements

PRACTISE *KNOW IT!*

 Skills introduced in Chapter 5:
- Practising notice it, note it, know it
- The pause practice

Skills introduced in Chapter 6:
- Exploring my self
- Identifying personal phrases

 Skills introduced in Chapter 7:
- Finding zest for life

PRACTISE *EMBRACE IT!*

 Skills introduced in Chapter 8:
- Awareness of thoughts
- Reframing ageing

 Skills introduced in Chapter 9:
- Exploring thoughts, emotions and physical sensations
- Exploring pleasant, neutral and unpleasant sensations

 Skills introduced in Chapter 10:
- Meeting challenges with self-affection
- Loving kindness meditation (*mettā*)

PRACTISE ALL THE SKILLS IN THE AGEING UPWARDS FRAMEWORK

- Ageing upwards

NOTES

[1] *Embrace*, Collins dictionary. Available from: www.collins dictionary.com/dictionary/english/embrace

[2] S. Bates, *Lifespan is continuing to increase regardless of socioeconomic factors, Stanford researchers find*, Stanford News (6 November 2018). Available from: https://news.stanford.edu/2018/11/06/lifespan-increasing-people-live-65/

[3] *The new map of life*, Stanford Center on Longevity. Available from: https://longevity.stanford.edu/the-new-map-of-life-report/

[4] This is the ratio of young and old dependent people (aged 15 and under as well as 65 and over) to the working-age population (aged 15–64). The figures are from: *Population structure and ageing*, Eurostat Statistics Explained. Available from: https://ec.europa.eu/eurostat/statistics-explained/index.php?title=Population_structure_and_ageing#Slightly_more_than_three_persons_of_working_age_for_every_person_aged_65_or_over

[5] The term was first used in R. Purser and D. Loy, *Beyond McMindfulness*, HuffPost (2013). Available from: www.huffpost.com/entry/beyond-mcmindfulness_b_3519289. It also appears in the title of Ron Purser's *McMindfulness: How mindfulness became the new capitalist spirituality* (Repeater, 2019).

[6] MBSR was developed by Jon Kabat-Zinn.

[7] Y-Y. Tang, Y. Ma, Y. Fan, H. Feng, J. Wang, S. Feng, Q. Lu, B. Hu, Y. Lin, J. Li, Y. Zhang, Y. Wang, L. Zhou and M. Fan, 'Central and autonomic nervous system interaction is altered by short-term

meditation' in *Proceedings of the National Academy of Sciences of the United States of America*, 106 (22), 8865–8870 (2009).

[8] D. Goleman and R.J. Davidson, *The science of meditation: How to change your brain, mind and body* (Penguin Life, 2017).

[9] D.G. Blanchflower, 'Is happiness U-shaped everywhere? Age and subjective well-being in 145 countries' in *Journal of Population Economics*, 34 (2), 575–624 (2021).

[10] C. Graham, *Happiness around the world: The paradox of happy peasants and miserable millionaires* (Oxford University Press, 2009).

[11] J. Tseng and J. Poppenk, 'Brain meta-state transitions demarcate thoughts across task contexts exposing the mental noise of trait neuroticism' in *Nature Communications*, 11: 3480 (2020).

[12] After School, *Life is NOT a journey – Alan Watts*, YouTube. Available from: https://youtu.be/rBpaUICxEhk

[13] *How and why do we age?*, Max Planck Institute for Biology of Ageing. Available from: www.age.mpg.de/healthy-ageing/how-and-why-do-we-age

[14] T.B.L. Kirkwood and S. Melov, 'On the programmed/non-programmed nature of ageing within the life history' in *Current Biology*, 21 (18), R701–R707 (2011).

[15] The nine hallmarks of ageing are genomic instability, telomere attrition, epigenetic alterations, loss of proteostasis, deregulated nutrient sensing, mitochondrial dysfunction, cellular senescence, stem cell exhaustion and altered intercellular communication. See C. López-Otín, A. Blasco, L. Partridge, M. Serrano and G. Kroemer, 'The hallmarks of aging' in *Cell*, 153 (6), 1194–1217 (2013).

[16] B. Newcomb, Incorporating social and behavioral factors alongside biological mechanisms is critical for improving aging research, says University Professor Eileen Crimmins, USC Leonard Davis School of Gerontology (2020). Available from: https://gero.usc.edu/2020/12/03/usc-aging-biology-social-factors/

[17] *Health*, Merriam-Webster.com Dictionary. Available from: www. merriam-webster.com/dictionary/health?src=search-dict-box

[18] M.A. von Faber, A. Bootsma-van der Wiel, E. van Exel, J. Gussekloo, A.M. La-gaay, E. van Dongen, D.L. Knook, S. van der Geest and R.G.J. Westendorp, 'Successful aging in the oldest old: Who can be characterized as successfully aged?' in *Archives of Internal Medicine*, 161 (22), 2694–2700 (2001).

[19] G.L. Albrecht and P.J. Devlieger, 'The disability paradox: High quality of life against all odds' in *Social Science & Medicine*, 48 (8), 977–988 (1999).

[20] It should be noted that in a 2020 study of well-being among individuals aged 60 and over in the United States, 33% of all older adults reported that they experience multidimensional well-being, while only 4–18% of older adults with disabilities said they experience well-being in the dimensions of material well-being, health status and personal activities. However, they experienced as much well-being as persons without disabilities in terms of health insurance status and social connections/relationships. See S. Mitra, D.L. Brucker and K.M. Jajtner, 'Well-being at older ages: Towards an inclusive and multidimensional measure' in *Disability and Health Journal*, 13 (4): 100926 (2020).

[21] A. Officer, J.A. Thiyagarajan, M.L. Schneiders, P. Nash and V. de la Fuente-Núñez, 'Ageism, healthy life expectancy and population ageing: How are they related?' in *International Journal of Environmental Research and Public Health*, 17 (9): 3159 (2020).

[22] *Global report on ageism*, World Health Organization. Available from: www.who.int/teams/social-determinants-of-health/demo graphic-change-and-healthy-ageing/combatting-ageism/global-report-on-ageism

[23] The number is for persons aged 65 and over in 2020. See United Nations Department of Economic and Social Affairs, Population Division, *World Population Ageing 2020: Highlights* (2020). Available from: www.un.org/development/desa/pd/sites/

www.un.org.development.desa.pd/files/undesa_pd-2020_world_population_ageing_highlights.pdf

[24] *Constitution*, World Health Organization. Available from: www.who.int/about/governance/constitution

[25] E.J. Lenze, S. Hickman, T. Hershey, L. Wendleton, K. Ly, D. Dixon, P. Doré and J.L. Wetherell, 'Mindfulness-based stress reduction for older adults with worry symptoms and co-occurring cognitive dysfunction', in *International Journal of Geriatric Psychiatry*, 29 (10), 991–1000 (2014).

[26] W.J. Rejeski, 'Mindfulness: Reconnecting the body and mind in geriatric medicine and gerontology' in *Gerontologist*, 48 (2), 135–141 (2008).

[27] S. Ernst, J. Welke, C. Heintze, R. Gabriel, A. Zollner, S. Kiehne, U. Schwantes and T. Esch, 'Effects of mindfulness-based stress reduction on quality of life in nursing home residents: A feasibility study' in *Forsch Komplementmed*, 15 (2), 74–81 (2008).

[28] A.M. Gallegos, J. Moynihan and W.R. Pigeon, 'A secondary analysis of sleep quality changes in older adults from a randomized trial of an MBSR program', in *Journal of Applied Gerontology*, 37 (11), 1327–1343 (2018).

[29] C.M. Smart, S.J. Segalowitz, B.P. Mulligan, J. Koudys and J.R. Gawryluk, 'Mindfulness training for older adults with subjective cognitive decline: Results from a pilot randomized controlled trial' in *Journal of Alzheimer's Disease*, 52 (2), 757–774 (2016).

[30] J.D. Creswell, M.R. Irwin, L.J. Bucklund, M.D. Lieberman, J.M.G. Arevalo, J. Ma, E.C. Breen and S.W. Cole, 'Mindfulness-based stress reduction training reduces loneliness and pro-inflammatory gene expression in older adults: A small randomized controlled trial', in *Brain, Behavior, and Immunity*, 26 (7), 1095–1101 (2012).

[31] D.C. Parra, J.L. Wetherell, A. Van Zandt, R.C. Brownson, J. Abhishek and E.J. Lenze, 'A qualitative study of older adults'

perspectives on initiating exercise and mindfulness practice' in *BMC Geriatrics*, 19 (1): 354 (2019).

[32] S.Y.H. Li and D. Bressington, 'The effects of mindfulness-based stress reduction on depression, anxiety, and stress in older adults: A systematic review and meta-analysis' in *International Journal of Mental Health Nursing*, 28 (3), 635–656 (2019).

[33] O. Klimecki, N.L. Marchant, A. Lutz, G. Poisnel, G. Chételat and F. Collette, 'The impact of meditation on healthy ageing – the current state of knowledge and a roadmap to future directions' in *Current Opinion in Psychology*, 28, 223–228 (2019).

[34] For instance, there is ongoing research into how mindfulness can influence the length of telomere. Meditation has also been found to reduce inflammation, which is something that is so closely linked to our biological ageing process that researchers came up with the term 'inflammaging'.

[35] A.M. van Loon, M.F.I.A. Depla, C.M.P.M. Hertogh, M. Huisman and A.A.L. Kok, 'The disability paradox? Trajectories of well-being in older adults with functional decline' in *Journal of Aging and Health*, 35 (1–2), 125–137 (2022).

[36] An excellent entry point to the research into functional contextualism can be found in S. Hayes, *State of the ACT evidence*, Association for Contextual Behavioral Science. Available from: https://contextualscience.org/state_of_the_act_evidence

[37] *The Global Health Observatory, Healthy life expectancy (HALE) at birth (years)*, WHO. Available from: www.who.int/data/gho/data/indicators/indicator-details/GHO/gho-ghe-hale-healthy-life-expectancy-at-birth

[38] *Life expectancy*, Statistics Netherlands (CBS). Available from: https://longreads.cbs.nl/european-scale-2019/life-expectancy/

[39] L.M. Fabbri and K.F. Rabe, 'From COPD to chronic systemic inflammatory syndrome?' in *Lancet*, 370 (9589), 797–799 (2007).

[40] Y. Chen, Y. Peng and P. Fang, 'Emotional intelligence mediates the relationship between age and subjective well-being' in *International Journal of Aging & Human Development*, 83 (2), 91–107 (2016).

[41] N.J. Shook, C. Ford, J. Strough, R. Delaney and D. Barker, 'In the moment and feeling good: Age differences in mindfulness and positive affect' in *Translational Issues in Psychological Science*, 3 (4), 338–347 (2017).

[42] For instance, see: L.C. Hohaus and J. Spark, 'Getting better with age: Do mindfulness & psychological well-being improve in old age?' in *European Psychiatry*, 28 (1) (2013); C.T. Mahoney, D.L. Segal and F.L. Coolidge, 'Anxiety sensitivity, experiential avoidance, and mindfulness among younger and older adults: Age differences in risk factors for anxiety symptoms' in *The International Journal of Aging & Human Development*, 81 (4), 217–240 (2015).

[43] M.A. Killingsworth and D.T Gilbert, 'A wandering mind is an unhappy mind' in *Science*, 330 (6006), 932 (2010).

[44] C.J. Norris, D. Creem, R. Hendler and H. Kober, 'Brief mindfulness meditation improves attention in novices: Evidence from ERPs and moderation by neuroticism' in *Frontiers in Human Neuroscience*, 12: 315 (2018).

[45] N. Kurmi, K. Bhagyalakshmi and R.D. Kini, 'Effect of mindfulness meditation on attention and working memory in elderly people' in *Indian Journal of Clinical Anatomy and Physiology*, 6 (1), 73–76 (2019).

[46] See, for instance: G. Robertson and R. Litherland, 'Mindfulness meditation: Can it make a difference?' in *The Journal of Dementia Care*, 22, 31–33 (2014); W.P. Wong, J. Coles, R. Chambers, D.B. Wu and C. Hassed, 'The effects of mindfulness on older adults with mild cognitive impairment' in *Journal of Alzheimer's Disease Reports*, 1 (1), 181–193 (2017).

[47] Y. Chen, J. Zhang, T. Zhang, L. Cao, Y. You, C. Zhang, X. Liu and Q. Zhang, 'Meditation treatment of Alzheimer disease and mild cognitive impairment: A protocol for systematic review' in *Medicine (Baltimore)*, 99 (10): e19313 (2020).

[48] P. Lorenz-Spreen, B.M. Mønsted, P. Hövel and S. Lehmann, 'Accelerating dynamics of collective attention' in *Nature Communications*, 10: 1759 (2019).

[49] C.L. Grady, M.V. Springer, D. Hongwanishkul, A.R. McIntosh and G. Winocur, 'Age-related changes in brain activity across the adult lifespan' in *Journal of Cognitive Neuroscience*, 18 (2), 227–241 (2006).

[50] S. Fountain-Zaragoza and R.S. Prakash, 'Mindfulness training for healthy aging: Impact on attention, well-being, and inflammation' in *Frontiers in Aging Neuroscience*, 9: 11 (2017).

[51] W.D. Stevens, L. Hasher, K.S. Chiew and C.L. Grady, 'A neural mechanism underlying memory failure in older adults' in *Journal of Neuroscience*, 28 (48), 12820–12824 (2008).

[52] For more information, see the Vipassana Meditation website (www.dhamma.org).

[53] J. Kabat-Zinn, *Wherever you go, there you are: Mindfulness meditation in everyday life* (Hyperion, 1994), p. 4.

[54] M. Csikszentmihalyi, *Flow: The psychology of optimal experience* (Harper and Row, 1990).

[55] T.D. Wilson, D.A. Reinhard, E.C. Westgate, D.T. Gilbert, N. Ellerbeck, C. Hahn, C.L. Brown and A. Shaked, 'Just think: The challenges of the disengaged mind' in *Science*, 345 (6192), 75–77 (2014).

[56] D. Kahneman, *Thinking, fast and slow* (Farrar, Straus and Giroux, 2013).

[57] R. Harris, *The struggle switch*, YouTube. Available from: https://youtu.be/rCp1l16GCXI

58 Dr. J. Bolte Taylor, *My stroke of insight* (Penguin, 2006).

59 I have not been able to validate whether Frankl actually said this.

60 C. Dovey, 'What old age is really like' in New Yorker (1 October 2015). Available from: www.newyorker.com/culture/cultural-comment/what-old-age-is-really-like

61 M.A. Harris, C.E. Brett, W. Johnson and I.J. Deary, 'Personality stability from age 14 to age 77 years' in *Psychology and Aging*, 31 (8), 862–874 (2016).

62 See K.M. Sheldon and S. Lyubomirsky, 'Revisiting the sustainable happiness model and pie chart: Can happiness be successfully pursued?' in *The Journal of Positive Psychology*, 16 (2), 145–154 (2021).

63 J. Anglim and S. Grant, 'Predicting psychological and subjective well-being from personality: Incremental prediction from 30 facets over the big 5' in *Journal of Happiness Studies*, 17 (1), 59–80 (2016).

64 S. Roccas, L. Sagiv, S.H. Schwartz and A. Knafo, 'The big five personality factors and personal values' in *Personality and Social Psychology Bulletin*, 28 (6), 789–801 (2002).

65 B.W. Roberts, J. Luo, D.A. Briley, P.I. Chow, R. Su and P.L. Hill, 'A systematic review of personality trait change through intervention' in *Psychological Bulletin*, 143 (2), 117–141 (2017).

66 P. Steel, J. Schmidt and J. Shultz, 'Refining the relationship between personality and subjective well-being' in *Psychological Bulletin*, 134 (1), 138–161 (2008).

67 J. Sun, S.B. Kaufman and L.D. Smillie, 'Unique associations between big five personality aspects and multiple dimensions of well-being' in *Journal of Personality*, 86 (2), 158–172 (2018).

68 N. Pornpattananangkul, A. Chowdhury, L. Feng and R. Yu, 'Social discounting in the elderly: Senior citizens are good

Samaritans to strangers' in *The Journals of Gerontology: Series B Psychological Sciences and Social Sciences*, 74 (1), 52–58 (2019).

[69] M.J. Poulin and C.M. Haase, 'Growing to trust: Evidence that trust increases and sustains well-being across the life span' in *Social Psychological and Personality Science*, 6 (6), 614–621 (2015).

[70] S. Scheibe and L.L. Carstensen, 'Emotional aging: Recent findings and future trends' in *The Journals of Gerontology: Series B Psychological Sciences and Social Sciences*, 65B (2), 135–144 (2010).

[71] N.W. Hudson, *Personality trait development and social investment in work* (Master's thesis, University of Illinois at Urbana Champaign, 2011). Available from: https://core.ac.uk/download/pdf/4834216.pdf

[72] D. Goleman and R.J. Davidson, *The science of meditation: How to change your brain, mind and body* (Penguin Life, 2017).

[73] K.D. Le Nguyen, J. Lin, S.B. Algoe, M.M. Brantley, S.L. Kim, J. Brantley, S. Salzberg and B.L. Fredrickson, 'Loving-kindness meditation slows biological aging in novices: Evidence from a 12-week randomized controlled trial' in *Psychoneuroendocrinology*, 108, 20–27 (2019).

[74] A. Steptoe and D. Fancourt, 'Leading a meaningful life at older ages and its relationship with social engagement, prosperity, health, biology, and time use' in *Proceedings of the National Academy of Sciences of the United States of America*, 116 (4), 1207–1212 (2019).

[75] E. Cumming and W.E. Henry, *Growing old* (New York, 1961).

[76] R.C. Atchley, 'Activity theory' in R. Schulz (ed.) *The encyclopedia of aging, fourth edition, volume 1: A–K* (Springer Publishing Company, 2006), pp. 9–13.

[77] P. Gilbert, *The compassionate mind: A new approach to life's challenges* (New Harbinger, 2009).

[78] R.G. Westendorp and F.H. Schalkwijk, 'When longevity meets vitality' in *Proceedings of Nutrition Society*, 73 (3), 407–412 (2014).

[79] R.G. Westendorp and F.H. Schalkwijk, 'When longevity meets vitality' in *Proceedings of Nutrition Society*, 73 (3), 407–412 (2014), p. 410.

[80] S. Oishi and E.C. Westgate, 'A psychologically rich life: Beyond happiness and meaning' in *Psychological Review*, 129 (4), 790–811 (2021).

[81] L.L. Besser and S. Oishi, 'The psychologically rich life' in *Philosophical Psychology*, 33 (8), 1053–1071 (2020).

[82] P. Dalby, 'Is there a process of spiritual change or development associated with ageing? A critical review of research' in *Aging and Mental Health*, 10 (1), 4–12 (2006).

[83] A. Zubko, *Treasury of spiritual wisdom* (Blue Dove Foundation, 1998), p. 338.

[84] H. Lavretsky, 'Spirituality and aging' in *Aging Health*, 6 (6), 749–769 (2010).

[85] L. Tornstam, 'Maturing into gerotranscendence' in *The Journal of Transpersonal Psychology*, 43 (2), 166–180 (2011), p. 168.

[86] L. Tornstam, 'Maturing into gerotranscendence' in *The Journal of Transpersonal Psychology*, 43 (2), 166–180 (2011).

[87] See L. Tornstam, 'Maturing into gerotranscendence' in *The Journal of Transpersonal Psychology*, 43 (2), 166–180 (2011), p. 172.

[88] B.R. Levy, M.D. Slade, S.R. Kunkel and S.V. Kasl, 'Longevity increased by positive self-perceptions of aging' in *Journal of Personality and Social Psychology*, 83 (2), 261–270 (2002).

[89] B. Levy, *Breaking the age code: How your beliefs about aging determine how long and well you live* (HarperCollins, 2022).

[90] J.E. Graham, L.M. Christian and J.K. Kiecolt-Glaser, 'Stress, age, and immune function: Toward a lifespan approach' in *Journal of Behavioral Medicine*, 29 (4), 389–400 (2006).

[91] If you don't believe me, read psychologist and winner of the Nobel Prize in economics Daniel Kahneman's *Thinking fast and slow* (Penguin, 2011).

[92] See, for instance, B. Fredrickson, *Positivity: Groundbreaking research reveals how to embrace the hidden strength of positive emotions, overcome negativity, and thrive* (Crown Publishers, 2009).

[93] B. Levy, *Breaking the age code: How your beliefs about aging determine how long and well you live* (HarperCollins, 2022).

[94] See, for instance: L.L. Carstensen, M. Pasupathi, U. Mayr and J.R. Nesselroade, 'Emotional experience in everyday life across the adult life span' in *Journal of Personality and Social Psychology*, 79 (4), 644–655 (2000); V. Orgeta, 'Specificity of age differences in emotion regulation' in *Aging & Mental Health*, 13 (6), 818–826 (2009); F. Blanchard-Fields, R. Stein and T.L. Watson, 'Age differences in emotion-regulation strategies in handling everyday problems' in *The Journals of Gerontology: Series B Psychological Sciences and Social Sciences*, 59 (6), P261–P269 (2004).

[95] J.L. Horn and R.B. Cattell, 'Age differences in fluid and crystallized intelligence' in *Acta Psychologica*, 26, 107–129 (1967).

[96] R.B. Zajonc, 'Attitudinal effects of mere exposure' in *Journal of Personality and Social Psychology*, 9 (2, Pt. 2), 1–27 (1968).

[97] A.E. Reed and L.L. Carstensen, 'The theory behind the age-related positivity effect' in *Frontiers in Psychology*, 3: 339 (2012).

[98] E.D. Tifft, S. Underwood, M.Z. Roberts and J.P. Forsyth, 'Using meditation in a control vs. acceptance context: A preliminary evaluation of relations with anxiety, depression, and indices of well-being' in *Journal of Clinical Psychology*, 78 (7), 1407–1421 (2022).

[99] See, for instance: T.B. Kashdan, V. Barrios, J.P. Forsyth and M.F. Steger, 'Experiential avoidance as a generalized psychological vulnerability: Comparisons with coping and emotion regulation strategies' in *Behaviour Research and Therapy*, 44 (9), 1301–1320

(2006); A.J. Shallcross, A.S. Troy, M. Boland and I.B. Mauss, 'Let it be: Accepting negative emotional experiences predicts decreased negative affect and depressive symptoms' in *Behaviour Research and Therapy*, 48 (9), 921–929 (2010); M.M. Linehan, K.A. Comtois, A.M. Murray, M.Z. Brown, R.J. Gallop, H.L. Heard and N. Lindenboim, 'Two-year randomized trial and follow-up of dialectical behavior therapy vs therapy by experts for suicidal behaviors and borderline personality disorder' in *Archives of General Psychiatry*, 63 (7), 757–766 (2006); S.H. Ma and J.D. Teasdale, 'Mindfulness-based cognitive therapy for depression: Replication and exploration of differential relapse prevention effects' in *Journal of Consulting and Clinical Psychology*, 72 (1), 31–40 (2004); M.P. Twohig, S.C. Hayes, J.C. Plumb, L.D. Pruitt, A.B. Collins, H. Hazlett-Stevens and M.R. Woidneck, 'A randomized clinical trial of acceptance and commitment therapy versus progressive relaxation training for obsessive compulsive disorder' in *Journal of Consulting and Clinical Psychology*, 78 (5), 705–716 (2010); L. Campbell-Sills, D.H. Barlow, T.A. Brown and S.G. Hofmann, 'Effects of suppression and acceptance on emotional responses of individuals with anxiety and mood disorders' in *Behaviour Research and Therapy*, 44 (9), 1251–1263 (2006); S.G. Hofmann, S.S. Heering and A. Asnaani, 'How to handle anxiety: The effects of reappraisal, acceptance, and suppression strategies on anxious arousal' in *Behaviour Research and Therapy*, 47 (5), 389–394 (2009); L. Campbell-Sills, D.H. Barlow, T.A. Brown and S.G. Hofmann, 'Acceptability and suppression of negative emotion in anxiety and mood disorders' in *Emotion*, 6 (4), 587–595 (2006).

[100] A.J. Shallcross, B.Q. Ford, V.A. Floerke and I.B. Mauss, 'Getting better with age: The relationship between age, acceptance, and negative affect' in *Journal of Personality and Social Psychology*, 104 (4), 734–749 (2013).

[101] R. Duncan, R. Francis, J. Collerton, K. Davies, C. Jagger, A. Kingston, T. Kirkwood, L. Robinson and F. Birrell, 'Prevalence of arthritis and joint pain in the oldest old: Findings from the Newcastle 85+ study' in *Age and Ageing*, 40 (6), 752–755 (2011).

[102] A. Abdulla, N. Adams, M. Bone, A.M. Elliott, J. Gaffin, D. Jones, R. Knaggs, D. Martin, L. Sampson and P. Schofield, 'Guidance on the management of pain in older people' in *Age and Ageing*, 42 (Suppl. 1), i1–i57 (2013).

[103] *Mindfulness meditation reduces pain by separating it from the self*, Science Daily (8 July 2022). Available from: www.sciencedaily.com/releases/2022/07/220708162754.htm

[104] A. Steptoe, N. Owen, S.R. Kunz-Ebrecht and L. Brydon, 'Loneliness and neuroendocrine, cardiovascular, and inflammatory stress responses in middle-aged men and women' in *Psychoneuroendocrinology*, 29 (5), 593–611 (2004).

[105] D. Umberson and J.K. Montez, 'Social relationships and health: A flashpoint for health policy' in *Journal of Health and Social Behavior*, 51 (Suppl.), S54–S66 (2010).

[106] J. Holt-Lunstad, T.B. Smith and J.B. Layton, 'Social relationships and mortality risk: A meta-analytic review' in *PLoS Medicine*, 7 (7): e1000316 (2010).

[107] N.R. Longrich, *The origin and evolution of love*, Britannica. Available from: www.britannica.com/story/the-origin-and-evolution-oflove

[108] K. Floyd, 'Relational and health correlates of affection deprivation' in *Western Journal of Communication*, 78 (4), 383–403 (2014).

[109] H. Tajfel, J.C. Turner, W.G. Austin and S. Worchel, 'An integrative theory of intergroup conflict' in M.J. Hatch and M. Schultz (eds) *Organizational Identity: A Reader* (Oxford University Press, 2004), pp. 56–65.

[110] *Gender ratio in the world*, Statistics Times (26 August 2021). Available from https://statisticstimes.com/demographics/world-sex-ratio.php

[111] Some studies have found a clear association between compassion and well-being. See, for instance: C. Schwartz, J.

Bell Meisenhelder, Y. Ma and G. Reed, 'Altruistic social interest behaviors are associated with better mental health' in *Psychosomatic Medicine*, 6 (5) 778–785 (2003); S.D. Pressman, T.L. Kraft and M.P. Cross, 'It's good to do good and receive good: The impact of a "pay it forward" style kindness intervention on giver and receiver well-being' in *Journal of Positive Psychology*, 10 (4), 293–302 (2014); S. Post, 'Altruism, happiness, and health: It's good to be good' in *International Journal of Behavioral Medicine*, 12 (2), 66–7 (2005).

112 B.L. Fredrickson, *Love 2.0: Finding happiness and health in moments of connection* (Plume, 2013).

113 L. Brown, J.C. Huffman and C. Bryant, 'Self compassionate aging: A systematic review' in *The Gerontologist*, 59 (4): e311e324 (2018). Other studies can be found on Kristin Neff's website (https://self-compassion.org/the-research/#areaofstudy).

114 U. Zessin, O. Dickhäuser and S. Garbade, 'The relationship between self-compassion and well-being: A meta-analysis' in *Applied Psychology: Health and Well-Being*, 7 (3), 340–364 (2015).

115 D. Surkalim, 'The prevalence of loneliness across 113 countries: Systematic review and meta-analysis' in *BMJ*, 376: e067068 (2022).

116 WHO, *Social isolation and loneliness among older people: Advocacy brief* (WHO, 2021). Available from: www.who.int/publications/i/item/9789240030749

117 E.W. Dunn, L.B. Aknin and M.I. Norton, 'Prosocial spending and happiness: Using money to benefit others pays off' in *Current Directions in Psychological Science*, 23 (1), 41–47 (2014).

118 S. Post and J. Niemark, *Why good things happen to good people* (Broadway Books, 2007).

119 B. Simpson and R. Willer, 'Beyond altruism: Sociological foundations of cooperation and prosocial behavior' in *Annual Review of Sociology*, 41, 43–63 (2015).

[120] G.K. Saini, S.B. Haseeb, Z. Taghi-Zada and J.Y. Ng, 'The effects of meditation on individuals facing loneliness: A scoping review' in *BMC Psychology*, 9: 88 (2021).

[121] P. Baltes and M. Baltes, 'Psychological perspectives on successful aging: The model of selective optimization with compensation' in P. Baltes and M. Baltes (eds) *Successful Aging: Perspectives from the Behavioral Sciences* (Cambridge University Press, 1990), pp. 1–34.

[122] A.M. Freund and P.B. Baltes, 'Selection, optimization, and compensation as strategies of life management: Correlations with subjective indicators of successful aging' in *Psychology and Aging*, 13 (4), 531–543 (1998); M.C. Janke, J.S. Son and L.L. Payne, 'Self-regulation and adaptation of leisure activities among adults with arthritis' in *Activities, Adaptation & Aging*, 33 (2), 65–80 (2009); D. Jopp and J. Smith, 'Resources and life-management strategies as determinants of successful aging: On the protective effect of selection, optimization, and compensation' in *Psychology and Aging*, 21 (2), 253–265 (2006).

[123] A.M. Freund, 'Age-differential motivational consequences of optimization versus compensation focus in younger and older adults' in *Psychology and Aging*, 21 (2), 240–252 (2006).

[124] H.J. Klug and G.W. Maier, 'Linking goal progress and subjective well-being: A meta-analysis' in *Journal of Happiness Studies*, 16 (1), 37–65 (2015).

[125] Older workers are, for instance, less likely to be shortlisted for interviews, hired, offered training opportunities or promoted. See R.A. Posthuma and M.A. Campion, 'Age stereotypes in the workplace: Common stereotypes, moderators, and future research directions' in *Journal of Management*, 35 (1), 158–188 (2009).

[126] C.R. Snyder, *The psychology of hope: You can get there from here* (Free Press, 1994).

[127] Self-efficacy was proposed by the psychologist Albert Bandura. See A. Bandura, 'Self-efficacy: Toward a unifying theory of behavioral change' in *Psychological Review*, 84 (2), 191–215 (1977).

[128] D. Grembowski, D. Patrick, P. Diehr, M. Durham, S. Beresford, E. Kay and J. Hecht, 'Self-efficacy and health behavior among older adults' in *Journal of Health and Social Behavior*, 34 (2), 89–104 (1993).

[129] T. Kostka and V. Jachimowicz, 'Relationship of quality of life to dispositional optimism, health locus of control and self-efficacy in older subjects living in different environments' in *Quality of Life Research*, 19 (3), 351–361 (2010).

[130] J.W. Moore, 'What is the sense of agency and why does it matter?' in *Frontiers in Psychology*, 7: 1272 (2016).

[131] J. Mirowsky, 'Age and the sense of control' in *Social Psychology Quarterly*, 58 (1), 31–43 (1995).

[132] R. Marks, J.P. Allegrante and K. Lorig, 'A review and synthesis of research evidence for self-efficacy-enhancing interventions for reducing chronic disability: Implications for health education practice (part I)' in *Health Promotion Practice*, 6 (1), 37–43 (2005).

[133] See, for instance: W.J. Rejeski, 'Mindfulness: Reconnecting the body and mind in geriatric medicine and gerontology' in *Gerontologist*, 48 (2), 135–141 (2008); M. Scult, V. Haime, J. Jacquart, J. Takahashi, B. Moscowitz, A. Webster, J.W. Denninger and D.H. Mehta, 'A healthy aging program for older adults: Effects on self-efficacy and morale' in *Advances in Mind-Body Medicine*, 29 (1), 26–33 (2015).

[134] V.E. Frankl, *Man's search for meaning* (Pocket Books, 1997).

[135] S.L. Hutchinson and G. Nimrod, 'Leisure as a resource for successful aging by older adults with chronic health conditions' in *International Journal of Aging & Human Development*, 74 (1), 41–65 (2012).

INDEX

Note: Page numbers with an 'n' denote Notes.